Advance Praise for *Sinner*

"The *Confessions* of Saint Augustine it is not, but the grand theme is the same: searching, stumbling, salvation. In a style that perhaps only he could get away with, Lino's personal stories and honest approach to the faith in this delightful book made me laugh, reflect, and sometimes wince, all the while reminding me that we all fall short of what God calls us to be—but, more importantly, that God's grace and mercy in Jesus are always available to all who seek it! It's a bold admission to say you're a sinner. Even bolder to write about it. *Sinner* is a winner."
—Cardinal Timothy Dolan, Archbishop of New York

"Lino Rulli has the guts to write candidly about his struggles with his faith and, in the process, reminds us why Jesus came to call sinners—because we need him. In chapters that are by turns funny, irreverent, touching, inspiring, and always honest, *Sinner* speaks to everyone who, as Scripture says, 'misses the mark'—in other words, everyone."
—Father James Martin, S.J., author of *Between Heaven and Mirth: Why Joy, Humor, and Laughter Are at the Heart of the Spiritual Life*

"It's corny to say that 'I laughed...I cried,' but truth be told, I did both. *Sinner* captures one man's experience of faith, one that is shared by so many others. As the saying goes, 'Every saint has a past; every sinner has a future.'"
—Father Leo E. Patalinghug, S.T.L., host of *Grace Before Meals*; professor of pastoral theology, Mount St. Mary's Seminary.

"In *Sinner*, Lino Rulli does what he does best—he courageously says what most only have the audacity to think. This is not your typical 'Catholic read'—it's a celebration of lunacy, where reverence and irreverence are embroiled in the cosmic tug-of-war that began all the way back in Eden. Underlying all the craziness, however, is a soul who is authentically contemplating the role of God in his life, the pitfalls of faith, and the challenges of living 'the Catholic life' in modern culture. *Sinner* reveals not only Lino's pursuit of God...but God's pursuit of him, and of us all."
—Mark Hart, author of *Blessed Are the Bored in Spirit* and executive vice president, Life Teen

"*Sinner* is a book for everyone. I'm planning to buy one for my favorite atheist!"
—Erika, listener who won "Write Lino's Book Blurb" contest

"Lino Rulli shamelessly bares his soul in this wacky, winsome narrative of his path from organ-grinder's monkey to Emmy-award-winning media man. From laugh-out-loud descriptions to well-placed, entirely sincere nuggets of spiritual wisdom, Rulli disarms us as the world's most unlikely Catholic evangelist. Quirky, charming, shyly pious, yet never pietistic, Rulli edifies as he entertains. Get ready for something like Saint Augustine's *Confessions* meets *Mad* magazine!"
—Father Thomas D. Williams, L.C., theologian, author, and Vatican analyst for CBS News

Praise for Lino Rulli

"A radio host like Howard Stern, only guilt-ridden and confession-going."
—*The New York Times*

"He's a jerk."
—Ex-girlfriend

"Laugh with Lino Rulli and discover why he's so darned popular."
—*Catholic Digest*

"He owes me fifteen bucks."
—Best friend

"He has Letterman's sharp delivery and Stern's penchant for pushing boundaries. Yet Lino is also pious."
—*St. Anthony Messenger*

"Lino fights for all sinners, but usually stays bogged down with his own caseload."
—Lino's personal attorney

"Lino Rulli…has proved popular with young adult audiences."
—Catholic News Service

sinner

Lino Rulli

{The **Catholic Guy**'s
funny, feeble attempts
to be a faithful Catholic}

PUBLISHED BY ST. ANTHONY MESSENGER PRESS
CINCINNATI, OHIO

Cover and book design by Mark Sullivan
Cover images © Jeffrey Bruno

Library of Congress Cataloging-in-Publication Data
Rulli, Lino.
Sinner : the Catholic Guy's funny, feeble attempt to be a faithful Catholic / Lino Rulli.
p. cm.
ISBN 978-1-61636-039-9 (alk. paper)
1. Rulli, Lino. 2. Catholics—United States—Biography. I. Title.
BX4705.R72945
[A3 2011]
282.092—dc23
[B]
2011027816

ISBN 978-1-61636-039-9

Published by Servant Books,
an imprint of St. Anthony Messenger Press.
28 W. Liberty St.
Cincinnati, OH 45202
www.AmericanCatholic.org
www.ServantBooks.org

Printed in the United States of America
Printed on acid-free paper

12 13 14 15 5 4 3 2

Contents

Introduction

I've always wanted to write an inspirational book. A book that helps others. Something that brings people closer to God. I want to be your spiritual guide.

Unfortunately, I'm a mess. I haven't figured anything out.

Having me write a book about the Catholic faith is like having a really bad actor write a book about the craft of acting. (Speaking of which, why hasn't Pauly Shore written a book about acting yet?)

The only way I could wrap my head around writing this book was if I called it *Sinner*, because that sums me up.

And I knew I had come up with the right name when not one person disagreed with it. If I called it *The Catholic Guy's Path to Sainthood* or *Holy Lino's Guide to God*, there would have been protests in the street and the burning of my image in effigy.

But it seemed everyone could agree on one thing: I'm a sinner.

Pretty much every book I've read by a Catholic author is from the perspective of a fully converted person. They live some crazy, sinful life, then they convert and never look back. Or they lived a boring life and are now faithful. Either way, it seems they've got the whole faith thing figured out.

Well, that's not me. I'm a crazy, converted sinner. The lifestyle is tough—both on my liver and on my soul. The stories in this book aren't all from a time in my past before I "knew" God. I was born and raised

Catholic, and these are stories of doubt and stupidity *while* knowing Him.

You see, I believe everything the Church teaches. That puts me in a minority, in and of itself. I'm just not great at being *faithful* to everything the Church teaches.

I don't have a problem with doctrine or dogma. I have a problem with me.

I want to be more faithful, but I'm scared. Scared that I'll try and fail. And in some ways even more scared that I'll succeed. What if I become such a good, holy Catholic that I wouldn't really want to hang out with me? Down deep, I love God with all my heart, mind, and strength. But you'll have to take my word for it since you can't usually tell.

In truth, the only thing that keeps me from going completely crazy is the Catholic Church. I haven't always felt God's presence. In fact, I don't feel God's presence all that often. I feel alone lots of days. But the Church has always been there. And that's where I've learned about God. Without the Church, I'd be a complete train wreck, not the small five-car derailment I am today.

So I want to write a book about the faith that touches your heart. That moves you and changes your life. But I don't know how to write that book.

Here's what I've got…

. . . . 1

Monkey Boy

"Lino, your mother and I have been talking," my dad said.

This raised red flags immediately. My parents never talked. Were they getting divorced? Was there an illness in the family? Would I finally find out I'm adopted?

"I've decided to leave my job as a parole officer to become an organ-grinder."

I stood there silent. Stunned. Primarily because I didn't know what an organ-grinder was. I didn't know what was happening to my dad. It sounded painful to have your organ ground. And to do the grinding yourself seemed stupid and foolhardy.

Al Gore had yet to invent the Internet, so I couldn't just Google the words *organ-grinder* and find out the real story: My dad was becoming the hurdy-gurdy man. Someone who cranks an organ, playing music, while a monkey dances around asking strangers for money.

Pops didn't make his announcement at the dinner table. In fact, we didn't own a dining room table. We ate at TV tables in front of, not surprisingly, the TV.

Neither did he make it at the weekly family meeting. Thankfully, we didn't have those. It was a small family—just me, my mom, and my dad—so it was pretty easy to get everyone together when necessary.

He made the announcement while leaving church. And not just the church which my dad attended only on Christmas and Easter. This announcement came in the summertime; Pops wouldn't normally be in church this time of year.

We were in Rome, Italy, on vacation, at St. Peter's Basilica, the greatest church ever built.

August, 1983. I was eleven years old and this, apparently, was the place where God told my dad to become an organ-grinder.

It's possible God really did speak to my dad, but I doubt it. God seems to speak in a crystal-clear way only to people He really likes. To the best of my knowledge, no one with the last name of *Rulli* has ever been in that group.

Nonetheless, God had a plan for my dad.

* * *

Some kids' dads have respectable jobs like lawyer or cop or proctologist. Some dads are admired for being IRS workers or hit men. I wouldn't be that lucky.

When asked in polite conversation what your father does for a living, few people in the past fifty years have answered with: "My dad? He's an organ-grinder." Try using that with your classmates. Or colleagues at work. Now you've entered my world.

It wasn't always this way, however. In fact, the first eleven years of my existence gave every impression that I would have a normal life. Mom was a high-school teacher. Pops was a corrections officer.

We were the only Catholic family on our block. There were the Lutherans and their Lutheran God. The Baptists and their Baptist God. The Seventh-Day Adventists and their…well, I was never sure what they believed. They were a very nice family, but they didn't give gifts for Christmas. That's a big no-no in a kid's eyes. You can believe whatever you want, but even my Jewish friends give gifts on Christmas.

My seemingly normal childhood was now changing. I was entering junior high, leaving my grade school classmates behind and preparing to meet a new group of people to reject me. I would soon be going through puberty, complete with faint mustache and bad mullet. It's possible I could survive those, but a father who was an organ-grinder? That put me in a whole other bracket.

My father's decision to change careers and forever alter his son's adolescence did not come overnight. It took my dad *several* nights to discern how best to interrupt my impending teenage years.

Perhaps he was looking out for his son's spiritual well-being. Certainly, chastity would not be a problem. Had my father chosen a respectable career—as a burglar or a con man, the type of family stock every girl dreams of—I could have forged ahead. As the son of the hurdy-gurdy man, however, I would spend a lot of time alone, chastely. As an added bonus, the family of an organ-grinder is traditionally not wealthy. I would embrace poverty at an early age. If I had learned to be obedient, I would have been on my way to a religious vocation.

* * *

If you ask my dad, becoming an organ-grinder was divinely mandated. Thus, I learned at a very early age that a person should discern God's will carefully.

If a saint has a private revelation, the Church investigates for years to determine the validity of this revelation. When your dad has a private revelation to become an organ-grinder, the Church is mysteriously silent.

According to Pops, he was in the Blessed Sacrament Chapel at St. Peter's, praying about it, and he felt at peace with the decision. And here's the thing I've found that sucks about other people's prayers: You can't really disagree with them. Well, you can, but the point is that the prayers are theirs, not yours, and as Christians, we do believe God speaks to us. So any time I question another person's prayer, I feel like the sinful, cynical person I'm afraid I am.

That's one of the truly weird things about Christianity: We believe God wants a relationship with us. That we talk and He listens and even answers.

Not in a big booming voice, though. Sometimes God speaks to us through others. Sometimes we feel an inner peace and know that He's answered. Sometimes we only *think* He's answered, like some moron televangelist who says, "God told me this or that," setting Christianity back hundreds of years.

Yet the scary thing is, God really does talk to us.

The lesson I learned is that if God calls my dad to be an organ-grinder, I have to accept it.

* * *

When my dad was a corrections officer in the early '80s, a friend of his decided to leave corrections to pursue his real dream of being a stand-up comedian.

This guy and my dad weren't best friends, just work buddies. My dad wished him well, and presumed this guy would be doing *Chuckles* in Fargo or *The Laugh Hut* in Tulsa for years to come.

It wasn't long after, however, that Pops and I were watching Johnny Carson on *The Tonight Show* and a comedian came out: Louie Anderson.

"That's my friend, Louie," Pops said. "Wow. He fulfilled his dream and made it as a comedian."

"Wait, Pops," I said, "you're friends with Louie Anderson?"

"Yeah, of course!" He paused and realized I'd soon be asking for celebrity swag.

"Well, not friends. But he interned for me in corrections."

The cat was out of the bag, though. I wanted to see if he really knew Louie.

For my birthday that year, Pops got me an autographed 8 x 10 photo of Louie Anderson. He wrote: "To Lino, I hope you have a wonderful life. Love, Louie."

I was happy to see my dad hadn't made the story up. At the same time, I was kinda hurt that Louie wanted to play no part in my life. He "hoped I had a wonderful life," but wasn't planning on finding out whether or not I did. Which made his claim of "love" at the end seem hollow.

Nonetheless, I think Louie's success helped inspire my dad to chase after his own dreams. Not a dream that would involve making millions, hosting *Family Feud*, and being a beloved figure. Nope, Pops just wanted to be the hurdy-gurdy man.

* * *

The majority of his weekends were spent at street fairs, grinding his organ for all to see. He'd play music, pose for pictures, and entertain the folks. Inevitably, however, a question would come from the crowd: "Hey, where's your monkey?!" An organ-grinder is nothing without a monkey. So Pops made a plan.

My dad sat me down to explain. "Lino, we can't get a monkey. First off, we can barely take care of the two cats in the house. Second, there's no room for a monkey around here. And third, we can't afford it. The insurance is too expensive. He could bite someone, they'd sue us, and we'd be stuck."

This all sounded like common sense. And I couldn't help but wonder if there were any other father–son conversations taking place on the planet at that moment about why the family couldn't get a monkey.

"OK, Pops," I said, thinking he just needed to get this information off his chest. As I got up to go, he stopped me.

"Since we can't get a real monkey…" There was a pause. Maybe he wanted me to figure it out on my own. Maybe his conscience was getting the better of him.

"I need you to dress up like a monkey and ask for money."

He got up and left the room, but walked back in with one more thought.

"Oh, and don't bite anyone or we'll get sued."

And with that, I became a monkey boy.

* * *

Now the majority of *our* weekends were spent at parades, county fairs, or standing on street corners—any place that wanted to see a guy grinding his organ. And there I was, cup in hand. Someone would drop a coin, or occasionally a dollar bill, in my cup.

"Thank you kindly," my dad would say. We never agreed on whether or not I should speak. Perhaps we'd make more money from the mute monkey boy.

I didn't wear a real monkey outfit, just a loose-fitting, long sleeve shirt and baggy stretch pants. I looked more like a gypsy than a monkey.

People got the point. I was *like* a monkey, in terms of my dance-around-and-hold-out-a-cup-for-money behavior. But it was also clear I was just doing the gig until my career as a waiter took off.

One Saturday afternoon, after a long, self-conscious day of this, Pops said we had more work that night.

"Lino, we've got a gig tonight I think you're gonna like," he said. This was actually good news because it meant I wouldn't just be sitting at home on a Saturday night. "It's downtown St. Paul."

I was a little nervous, imagining us roaming the gritty streets of the city, just my dad, me, and the organ.

"We're playing Prince's birthday party."

Mr. Purple Rain himself. This was at the height of his popularity. For once, I was actually looking forward to one of our gigs.

We were stationed at the front of the theater where the birthday party was held. We were the oddity entertainment, the musical accompaniment while you found out if you were on the guest list or not.

About an hour into the gig, my dad playing, me standing there quietly, Prince walked by.

"Hi," he said in his quiet little voice. "Thanks for being here."

"Happy birthday, Prince." It was weird calling him by name.

* * *

Some days I don't know what God's plan is for me or anyone else. Some days I'm frustrated about the lack of clarity in His plan, and the fact that everyone else seems to know God's will just makes me jealous.

But my dad has always been a great character, and I couldn't imagine him now as anything but an organ-grinder. Cranking that organ, he has brought joy to hundreds of thousands of people. Though it was at times pretty awkward for me, it's clear God had a plan. And it was a plan to bring peace to my dad.

Glad you became an organ-grinder, Pops. Whether God told you to or not.

. . . . 2

Cave Girl

I've got a soul, but I don't believe in soul mates. And I don't say that just because I'm thirty-nine and single.

I don't believe in soul mates because it just doesn't make theological sense. Our souls are complete the way they are. At the moment of conception, God places a unique and eternal soul in each person. We're not incomplete until meeting that other person. Someone else may add joy, but my soul is just fine being single.

And if soul mates did exist, with six billion people on the planet, what if my soul mate were on the other side of the world? How would I ever find her?

* * *

August, 2008. I met the most beautiful girl in the world. Big brown eyes. Long brown hair. Dark skin. She thought I was funny. She thought I was cute. And she was sober.

I walked by her as she was selling jewelry.

"Would you like to buy something for your girlfriend?" she asked.

"No girlfriend," I replied. [Sigh]

"What about for your wife?"

"Don't have a wife," I more sheepishly replied. [Internal sobbing]

"No wife, no life," she replied.

"Oh, that's pleasant," I said. "Been rehearsing that all day?"

She burst into a big laugh and showed her incredible smile.

"Where are you from?" she asked.

"New York," I replied, knowing it sounds much cooler to say you live there than to actually live there.

I looked at her goods. Her jewelry, that is. And every time I made a joke, she'd touch my left arm.

"I'll give you a good deal. I'll make an offer just for you."

For the record, I realize that when I enter a restaurant or bar, the female waitstaff are paid to be nice to me. I'm not a novice. I've been the recipient of women's attention in all forms of entertainment, whether they sit, stand, or dance. I'm supposed to be fooled into thinking they like me. I'm not fooled.

But this girl was different. I was different. So I spent ten dollars on jewelry for my mom and goddaughter. I wanted to get to know this beautiful woman better. Go on dates, get married, have kids, grow old together, that kind of thing. But here's the catch.

I was in the country of Jordan. Specifically, the city of Petra.

* * *

I'm an Indiana Jones fan. I loved *Raiders of the Lost Ark* and was an especially big fan of *Indiana Jones and the Last Crusade*. That's the one where Sean Connery played Indy's dad and they searched for the Holy Grail.

There's a scene in *Last Crusade* when they ride on horseback through a city whose buildings are carved out of rock. It's magical looking. The building in which they find the Holy Grail was one of the most incredible places I'd ever seen. I assumed it was created on a studio lot, but it's a real place: the city of Petra, Jordan.

The entire city was carved out of this rock two thousand years ago. Buildings, theaters, homes, you name it. The people who lived there are known as bedouins. For centuries, Petra was lost to most of the world, a period when no one except for the bedouin saw it. In the 1800s a dude came upon it and, I'm guessing, said: "You've gotta be kidding me!"

From Jordan's capital city of Amman, it's a three-hour drive to Petra. Once at the entrance to the city, it's a thirty-minute walk (cars are not allowed) to the building known as the treasury where they filmed *The Last Crusade*. If you go to the right of the treasury, find a short, narrow path with steps carved out of the rock, and climb up a mountain about forty-five minutes, you'll find a girl selling jewelry. My *not* soul mate.

* * *

So the girl I met is a bedouin. She lives in a cave. In fact, she showed me her cave, not far from Petra. It was as if I met a character from *The Flintstones*: Pebbles Flintstone. And that's what I called her because no matter how many times she told me her name I was unable to repeat it properly.

Pebbles spoke fluent English. She'd been around tourists her whole life, and she learned it from them. I asked what other languages she spoke, hoping to impress her with my world travels.

When I learned she spoke Italian, I said, "Ciao."

When I learned she spoke Chinese, I said, "Ni hao."

When I learned she spoke Japanese, I said, "Konnichiwa!"

And she found it all hilarious. Admittedly, she does live in a cave, so that may explain why she found this entertaining. Compared to tending goats, I come off as quite charming. But honestly, there was something more to it.

"I never have this kind of conversation with anyone," she said. And then she invited me for tea with her family. I was afraid it meant I was becoming a member of the family. Turns out it just meant drinking tea. Kinda like where I'm from.

"I want to give you a bracelet," she told me.

This made me wonder if I paid too much for the pieces of jewelry I bought, or if she actually wanted to give me something to remember her by. I'd like to think the latter. My little cave girl gave me a silver bracelet to remind me of her. And with that we said good-bye and I started my trek back down the mountain.

* * *

After walking down the beautifully carved steps of stone, I realized I had to see her again. I had seen too many PG-13 movies not to go back and tell her...something. I love you. I need you. I want to move to a cave. Something.

So in the ninety-five degree heat, I climbed back up the steps. A slow, sweaty, creepy walk. The minute our eyes met she greeted me with a huge smile. "What are you doing here?"

"I've gotta take a picture of you," I breathed heavily. "*With* you. I have to have a picture of the two of us."

In case you're wondering: Yes, she'd seen cameras before.

What a wonderful picture of two very different people. She lives in a cave. I live on the Upper West Side of Manhattan. My street address has numbers and a street name. Hers is something like the third cave on the right.

Pessimists would say she was my green-card soul mate. But let me put it this way: Most girls don't like me. But she seemed to like me. We had genuine chemistry. It was as if we were...well, you know. I can't say it.

We said good-bye and I walked back down the mountain, shaking my head, with only one question in my mind: "Why must you mock me, O Lord?"

* * *

The Bible says that God knew me before He formed me in the womb. I can't imagine a loving God who counts the hairs on my head, loves me, and then says: "I've created a soul mate for you. Good luck finding her."

And even though she wasn't my soul mate, I still really liked her.

. . . . 3

Late Show Without Lino Rulli

In the Jubilee Year of 2000, I went on a pilgrimage. While most Catholics celebrated two thousand years of Christianity by visiting holy cities and shrines, I went somewhere a little different. My pilgrimage was to New York City to see a guy with a late-night franchise: David Letterman.

I was working for CBS at the time, and other than the whopping eighteen dollars an hour I received as a television reporter, there was one other perk: the e-mail address of a woman who handled *Late Show* tickets for CBS employees.

After a quick correspondence, I got my tickets. Well, *ticket,* to be precise. I was on this pilgrimage by myself.

I flew from Minnesota to New York on a Sunday night and took the shuttle bus into the city. Coming over the Triborough Bridge and seeing the lights of the City That Never Sleeps was thrilling. The Empire State building. The Chrysler building. This was how the Christians of the Middle Ages must have felt when seeing Rome or Jerusalem for the first time.

I had been to New York only once before, back in 1987 with my dad. He had an acquaintance who knew someone who had a cousin who owned a flophouse in Brooklyn, so we stayed there for the two-day trip.

My father is extremely liberal except when it comes to spending money. He's all for Big Government spending, just not Big Rulli spending.

Other than the dismal housing, my only recollection of New York is of taking the NBC studio tour and seeing where *Late Night with David Letterman* was taped. Dave was on vacation that week so I couldn't see the man himself, but I saw the studio and bought a gray *Late Night* T-shirt. I wore it for so many years that the health department took it away from me.

Now I was returning to Dave's city, and it was just like he described it: New York smelled of urine, crime was rampant, there were prostitutes, drug dealers, and transients everywhere. And those were just the folks on the bus with me.

The shuttle dropped me off at my hotel on Eighth Avenue, I put my bags in the closet space the hotel billed as a room, and made my way up Broadway. I stood in front of the marquis of the Ed Sullivan Theater where Dave has done his show since 1993 and stared in awe.

* * *

The next day I reported at 2:00 PM for the taping. I stood in line, learned that seating would be random, and began to pray. "Oh God, please let me get a good seat." I'm the type who is never afraid to ask God for stuff, but I'm also good at prioritizing my prayers. When important things like Letterman seats come up, for example, I pray for a good seat and then apologize for my prior, wasted prayers. "Seriously, I'm sorry I asked for a good parking spot that time at IKEA. Or the time I prayed for a well-done steak. Those prayers weren't necessary. The seat thing is way more important."

Of course, it's not like He can take the parking spot or steak back from me; I'm just trying to let Him know that *this* is what I really want.

One of the pages for the show, a college kid no doubt desperately trying to get into showbiz, led us into the theater. I pushed a few old ladies out of the way, raced to the front row, and took my seat.

Another page came up and said, "You've got the best seat in the house." I felt it was an Anointed Trip.

First, the warm-up comedian, Eddie Brill, did a few minutes of material. Then, Paul Shaffer and the CBS Orchestra came out and started playing tunes. It was like seeing old friends.

Eddie then asked, "Are you ready to meet Dave?" and Letterman came sprinting out. I couldn't believe it. It was Dave Letterman. A guy I've admired my whole life. My television hero, in the flesh. And the thought suddenly occurred to me: "Why haven't I ever tried to work for this guy?"

* * *

From adolescence on, the only thing I was really interested in doing was comedy.

Every day after school, I raced home to watch the *Late Night with David Letterman* episode I had videotaped the night before. This was where my passions were. This was what I was excited about. Shouldn't a guidance counselor have noticed this odd behavior and encouraged me to follow my dreams?

Unfortunately, my guidance counselor was too busy lamenting the fact that he became a guidance counselor to actually help guys like me.

Here's how the conversation should have gone:

Guidance counselor, happy to help young people fulfill their God-given talents: "Well, Mr. Rulli, what are you passionate about?"

Young Lino Rulli: "I can make people laugh. And I love late-night television."

Middle-aged man, happy to make a difference in this world: "Perhaps God has given you these talents for a reason. How can you glorify God with them?"

Lino: "I don't know. But I love watching Dave Letterman. Maybe someday I can work with him, and explore my gifts and talents that way?"

Guy answering his own vocation in life by helping others: "Well, let's see about getting you an internship there. My research indicates that a number of folks on Dave's staff were interns, so that'd be a great place to start."

Instead, here's how the conversation actually went:

Middle-aged man, wishing he had done anything else with his life: "Well, what are you good at Lie-no [never taking the time to learn my name]?"

Young Lino Rulli: "I can make people laugh. And I love late-night television."

Guy who'd rather be lying in the middle of the freeway: "Yeah, well, we all like TV. And making people laugh is easy. *Alf* makes me laugh till I cry. But does making people laugh even pay?"

Lino: "Well, I don't know."

Guy counting down the days until his miserable existence will be over: "Well, good talk."

* * *

Sitting in the Ed Sullivan Theater, I finally realized: This is what I want to do with my life. I want to work for David Letterman.

Sadly, I realized this eleven years too late. I graduated high school in 1989. It was now 2000. I didn't think the Letterman show would be interested in a twenty-nine-year-old intern.

But was it too late? Almost definitely so. However, "with God all things are possible," the Bible says (Matthew 19:26), and that's the spirit in which Christians pray when it's definitely gonna take a miracle. Rarely is the with-God-all-things-are-possible perspective brought up when ordering a BLT or picking out an outfit for the day. Those things we feel are pretty possible on our own.

It took me three years to act on my realization that I wanted to be a writer for *The Late Show*. In 2003 I sent away for an application and discovered that, along with a resume, I had to submit three sample Top Ten Lists. The topics were as follows:

- *Top Ten Ways the World Would Be Different if a Dog Were President*
- *Top Ten Signs Your Gym Teacher Is Nuts*
- *Top Ten Things Overheard at Our First Show Fifteen Years Ago*

Below are my Top Ten Lists for the first two categories.

Top Ten Ways the World Would Be Different if a Dog Were President

10. Richard Nixon no longer the hairiest president in history.
9. Use of the word *bitch* appears in State of the Union address. (Also applies if Snoop Dogg were president.)
8. Have Kenneth Starr investigate what kind of meat is *really* being served at Chinese restaurants.
7. Replace C-Span with E-Span: All Ed Asner, all the time.
6. President determined by voters, versus being chosen by brother in Florida.
5. Tough new sentencing guidelines: three bites and you're out.
4. Secret Service nickname *horndog* not reserved for Bill Clinton anymore.
3. War on Terror replaced by War on Fleas and Ticks.
2. President: a Jack Russell. Vice President: a Nipsey Russell.
1. Bomb the crap out of Canada. They'll never know what hit 'em.

Top Ten Signs Your Gym Teacher Is Nuts

10. During batting practice, refers to ball as "Wendy, that tramp who broke my heart."
9. As prom-night chaperone, wears elegant strapless jockstrap.
8. Has athlete's foot on hands and forearms.
7. Ignoring U.N. warnings, invades foreign country searching for weapons of mass destruction.
6. That whistle around his neck? Actually a dog whistle.
5. When class plays softball, creepily asks which kids are "switch hitters."
4. When hitting the showers: shampoos, rinses, doesn't repeat.
3. Spikes Gatorade with Mad Dog 20/20.
2. Insists Gabe Kaplan is on the verge of a huge comeback.
1. Always willing to give you a hand with a groin pull.

You may have laughed; you may not have laughed. Though a few of the jokes are dated now, I thought I had what it takes to become a Letterman writer.

If you are in the may-not-have-laughed category, perhaps *you* have what it takes to become a Letterman writer. I was informed that *I* did not. A photocopied form letter arrived in the mail just a week later, presumably the same one sent to millions of wannabe Letterman writers like me. I don't remember the exact contents of the letter—I tore it up in a fit of rage—but it went something like this:

> *Dear Sir/Madam,*
>
> Thank you for submitting your application to work for *The Late Show*. Unfortunately, we are not currently hiring completely untalented dreamers. We wish you the best of luck on whatever planet you live on, under whatever misguided star

> led you to think you had a chance of working for one of your heroes.
>
> Sincerely,
>
> Person who *is,* in fact, working for one of your heroes

Not wanting to take no for an answer, however, I turned to prayer and remembered a verse in Scripture about a widow who annoyed the crap out of a judge (cf. Luke 18:1–5). Basically, the judge finally gave her what she wanted, not because he was just, but because he was afraid she would keep annoying him. Or she might even hit him.

With that biblical story rolling around in my brain, I decided to be persistent. Seek and I shall find, knock and the door will be answered, write and I shall be hired.

Taking this passage out of context, I came up with a new plan: Every week for three months I'd send the head writers of *The Late Show* my daily monologue jokes, scripted bits, and whatever other comedy I could come up with. This would show my talent and persistence. They'd have no choice but to bring me on staff.

My first step was to find stationery that would really stand out. I picked fluorescent yellow. They'd remember that.

Every Monday, week in and week out, I would write jokes, Top Ten Lists, and segments for the show. I realized they couldn't be used on the air, of course, but every once in a while I'd notice Dave do a joke that slightly resembled something I'd written and think to myself: "Keep going, Lino! They're reading your stuff! Maybe they're subliminally influenced by your work!"

Would it surprise you to find out that three months of sending letters in fluorescent envelopes resulted in a restraining order? Well, it wouldn't surprise me, either. Thankfully, that didn't happen. I'm guessing my letters got tossed in the garbage.

Four months in, I realized I was wasting my time. My dream of being a Letterman writer had to end. I was mad at God. I was mad at myself.

In retrospect, there were two fatal flaws to my plan:

First and foremost, I took the Bible out of context. It is a story about persistence in faith, not about harassing people until you get your way.

Second, it's not as if Letterman's head writers have nothing better to do than sit around and read lame comedy bits from strangers in the Midwest.

Unfortunately, however, in an effort to impress people, I had been telling everyone that I was being considered as a Letterman writer.

"We're in talks," I'd say. "I contacted them, they got back to me immediately, and I submitted a bunch of Top Ten Lists. They don't have any job openings right now, but we're still in touch on a weekly basis. I send them material, some of it gets on the air, and we'll see what happens."

When I realized the job would never come, I pulled the classic religious move: I determined it wasn't God's will.

"Hey Lino," someone would ask. "How's it going with Letterman's people?"

I'd answer piously, "Well, we've been in communication the past four months, but I've determined it's not God's will. And I'm at peace with that."

The truth is, I don't have what it takes to be a Letterman writer. To say "It's not God's will" is bringing God into a conversation that never took place.

If I want to be pope this year, it's not gonna happen. Yeah, I can say, "It just isn't God's will that I become the Roman pontiff," but even more, it's just not realistic. Hiding behind the not-God's-will excuse is the cop-out of all cop-outs.

I wish that Old Lino could talk to Young Lino and just say, "What do you enjoy doing and what are you good at? There's a pretty good chance God put those desires in you for a reason and you've got to figure that out." I'd be the guidance counselor I never had.

Lots of people put their failures in the not-God's-plan category instead of the I-suck-at-that category.

I don't need "The Top Ten Reasons Lino Will Never Work for David Letterman." The reason I'll never work for *The Late Show* is that I don't really have what it takes. That's why it's not God's plan.

4

Robert Johnson

Though it's not an infallible statement, I can say with some degree of certainty that guys named Jimmy are fun to hang out with. They'll usually get you in trouble, though.

Want to hang out with a guy named James? That's fine. Guys named Jimmy? That's another story.

I became friends with Jimmy my freshman year of college. He was a man's man. Had he lived a few hundred years ago, he'd be someone who challenged you to a duel—and always won. One night at a party, we were listening to Bobby Brown and drinking from a Coors Light party ball when some guy bumped into Jimmy.

"You got a problem, pal?" Jimmy asked.

The guy, apparently wanting to be beaten up, looked Jimmy in the eyes. "Yeah, I've got a problem. You."

"Well, let's go, man."

Like boxers at the beginning of a heavyweight match, they both had their fists up, waiting to see who would strike first.

The guy threw a punch and missed. Jimmy threw a punch and didn't. He connected directly with the guy's jaw, knocking him out. He lay on the ground, twitching. I was happy to be friends with the man not on the ground.

Jimmy was also my connection to a fake ID. Most every college kid wanted one, so I was thrilled when I heard that Jimmy could make them. A few of us headed down to our friend Paul's room, where Jimmy would take our photos in preparation for our new future of illegal underage drinking.

In the room was a large piece of cardboard, maybe two feet tall and three feet wide. At the top of this piece of cardboard, in bold block letters, it said *Nevada Driver's License*. It then listed a name, address, and everything you'd expect on a driver's license.

All we had to do was stand in front of the blank lower-right-hand corner.

It struck me as the type of thing you'd see at a modern art museum. "Oh, how deep, it's a life-sized driver's license."

It also struck me as something that would never work. I stood in front of the huge piece of cardboard and said, "Jimmy, there's no way this is going to look right!"

"Yeah, it will, Lino, trust me," he said with a smile, as he stood, Polaroid camera in hand, exactly two-and-a-half feet away in order to get just the right dimensions.

"But how..."

Flashbulb went off, picture taken. My fake ID photo was of me arguing with him about how *fake* my fake ID would look.

"Next!" Jimmy yelled, and another guy stepped up.

As friend after friend posed in front of the driver's license, I brought something up: "Hey, guys, let's think this through," I offered in a calm tone, trying to use reason. "First, the ID is for the state of Nevada. We live in Minnesota. How are we going to explain why a group of fifteen guys all moved from Nevada to a small Catholic university in Minnesota?"

Silence, except for the sound of another picture being taken.

"Next!" Jimmy yelled, as another friend stood in front of the license.

"Anyone have a problem with the fact that we all have the same address?" This time my tone was a little more aggressive. "If we go to a bar together, how do we explain why we all live in the same house?"

More silence. And another picture taken.

"Next!" Jimmy yelled.

I continued, "What about the fact that we all share the same birthday?" Again, silence.

The allure of a fake ID was too strong; reason didn't stand a chance. Sin has a way of blinding us…

Under my breath, I said aloud, "Should I even bring up the fact that we all share the same name?"

And yet, a few days later, it was official. I was Robert Johnson, resident of Nevada, and of legal drinking age.

As soon as we got the IDs, we tested them out. We headed to our favorite local college bar, and let's just say the bouncer wasn't the type to ask a lot of questions. We all got in.

Several hours into the night, the local cop showed up. A pitiable job, really, to go into small college bars and look for underage kids.

"How's it going?" the officer asked.

"Good," I slurred in return.

"Are you over twenty-one?"

"Yep."

"Can I see your ID?"

"Sure," as I handed him my fake ID I assumed he was as drunk as I was and wouldn't notice the errors. I had to admit, when I was drunk the thing looked just fine.

"You're from Nevada, huh?" he pondered. I knew things were going really well. He's buying it.

"Say, what's the capital of Nevada?" he asked. Great. A curious cop.

"I don't know," I replied. "I'm drunk." I thought he'd enjoy that.

"What's your address?"

"Don't remember," I said. "Haven't lived there in a while."

"What's your name?"

Suddenly I couldn't remember my name. I knew it was generic. But was I Robert Johnson or Robert Smith? I went with Smith.

"Do you have your *real* ID on you?"

At this point, I gave him my real ID showing I was a Minnesota resident, eighteen years old, named Angelo Rulli. He'd know I meant no harm. Maybe I could even buy him a beer.

He asked if I wanted to tell him who made my fake ID.

"I don't want to answer any questions until I speak with my lawyer," I replied.

We both had a good laugh about that.

"This is the third fake Nevada ID I've taken tonight," he said. "I'd love to know who made them."

Defiantly I responded: "Well, I'm not telling you. I'm not going to squeal. I'm no rat."

"I'm not going after the guy," the officer replied. "I just think you should ask for your money back."

We went to the police station, where I got my ticket for underage drinking and possession of a fake ID. My punishment was a fine and some community service, which was no big deal. I figured the incident was behind me.

It wasn't. The police notice arrived at my parents' house. Since I didn't actually live in Nevada and since my permanent address was my parents' home, that's where the letter went. And since my dad and I both share the same name, he opened it thinking it was for him. He was quite surprised to learn he was charged with possessing a fake ID. He called my dorm room and left a message.

"Lino, it's Pops," I heard when I checked my messages. At first I was afraid something had happened to them or a loved one. "I've got a letter here in the mail about a fake ID." And then I realized something *was* going to happen to a loved one: me.

"What the hell is going on?" he said, the cheap answering machine making his voice sound like he was so mad he was shaking. "If you think…"

I hit *stop*. Might as well call him and hear it in person. He answered on the first ring.

"Hello?" my dad said.

"Hey, Pops, it's…"

Before I could get a sentence out, he began with a life lesson: "This is what they mean by saying drinking costs money. It's not just the booze. It's the legal fees."

"Well, actually," I argued, "I've spent thousands on alcohol, but when it comes to fines, I've only spent a few hundred dollars. That means…"

"Oh, shut up. Here's your mother."

"Lino?" she asked, sounding as sad as if I'd been kidnapped and was being held hostage. "How are you?"

"Mom, I'm fine. I got busted with a fake ID, that's all."

"Oh, well, because when your father opened up the letter…"

At this point I realized I'm in for a second-by-second account of every emotion experienced and word uttered from the moment they got the letter to the beginning of this conversation. Ten minutes later, she wrapped up:

"…and that's when your father handed the phone to me."

I saw an opening to talk: "Right, Mom, I know. Sorry."

"We just want the best for you."

My parents still loved me. They forgave me. I could feel that love, even though I didn't deserve it. At least, I felt that love from my mom. With Pops, I sometimes felt like the jury was still out.

And I try to remember that that's the type of love God has for me. Even greater.

God loves me in spite of my sins. I can push Him away, but He's always wanting to take me back. God's love is there in my weaknesses and sins and stupid mistakes. As St. John Bosco said: "God, in His infinite goodness, puts up with us."

* * *

A few months later, fake-ID-less, my friends and I decided to go to a small college town in northern Minnesota, a few hours' drive away. Our friend Will was going to school there, and we had heard that it was a good place to drink without an ID.

On our first night in town, the six of us went to a house party where, for three bucks, we'd get all the beer we could drink. But that wasn't enough for us. We also thought we should steal some food. Even though the people throwing the party were fellow college kids who needed their cans of tuna fish and baked beans, we took a few of each and left the party—after drinking as much of their beer as possible, of course.

On the way home from the house party, Will came up with an idea.

"See that abandoned warehouse there?" he asked. Obviously we could see it; we weren't *that* drunk. "Let's see who can hit the window!"

We were about fifty feet from the building, and Will's first throw didn't hit the window. In fact, it didn't even hit the building.

"Let's go up closer," he said. "It's too far away." Couldn't be his arm, of course.

His second throw hit the building, but not the window.

We walked much closer—we were now maybe ten feet away—and he heaved another can of beans at the building. This one couldn't miss. It went through a window and an alarm rang. Apparently the warehouse wasn't abandoned.

We ran, zigzagging through lawns, alleys, and side streets for about ten minutes until we felt we were in the clear. Imagine our surprise, then, when a squad car pulled up and jumped the curb onto the sidewalk to cut us off.

An officer rolled out, T.J. Hooker–style, and realized he wasn't facing some hardened criminals, just six drunk college kids slightly out of breath.

"There's been a report of some vandalism. You guys wouldn't have some canned goods on you, would you?"

As he spoke, a second squad car pulled up and a cop jumped out, presumably unaware of the historically strange question the officer had asked us.

Thankfully, we could be honest. Will spoke first: "No. No canned goods here, Officer."

What we were all thinking, of course, is that we didn't have any canned goods because he had thrown them all into—or near—the warehouse.

"You guys at a party tonight?"

"Yes, Officer, we were, but it was a dud," one of my other friends offered.

"Well," the officer said, "we're heading to a house party right now. Get in the car."

He put three of us in one patrol car, the other three in the other. For a moment I thought this was northern Minnesotan hospitality, bringing visitors to college parties. Then it occurred to me: He was able to trace us to the party and was bringing us to the home of the now canned-goods-less college guys.

We sat in the back of the car as the officer went inside and brought the owners of the home out to us.

"Are these the guys who stole your food?" he asked them. One of the guys made eye contact with me, and the look in his eye said he wanted to turn us in. The only problem was this: If he said that we stole their food, he'd be admitting they served alcohol to minors and we'd all be going to jail.

"Nope," they said, frustrated. "These aren't the guys."

The cops had to charge us with something, though.

"We're bringing you to jail," the officer said.

I started to laugh. "What are the charges?"

"Well, vandalism. And underage drinking."

"But, Officer, we haven't been found guilty of either of those."

"Have you been drinking?"

"Yes."

"Are you underage?"

"Yes."

"So that's why you're going to jail."

"But you didn't know those facts till I just told you!"

"Did you vandalize a building?"

"No."

"OK, one out of two ain't bad. Just thought I'd try to get you."

We drove from the party and headed to jail. But he seemed to have loosened up and was at least smiling as we drove.

"Any chance we can stop to get something to eat?" I asked.

"No."

"Come on, you've gotta be hungry. I'm not saying a donut place. Just like an omelet or something. Everyone likes breakfast late at night, no?"

"I haven't been drinking, like you guys."

Fifteen minutes later, we arrived at the jail.

"OK, boys," the cop said, "time for the breathalyzer."

The moment of truth had come. We all knew we would fail so at this point it became a competition to see who would win. I did, with a .19, keeping in mind that .08 at the time was legally drunk. We were charged and put in a cell.

On the counsel of my publisher, lawyer, and spiritual director, I'm not allowed to share the tales of that night. But I'm allowed to discuss the fallout.

* * *

My license was revoked the following month, and I had to take an alcohol awareness class. I thought the class name was ironic, though, since it was obvious I was *aware* of alcohol. Within six months, I'd been arrested twice because of the stuff. My problem wasn't awareness, my problem was getting caught. I'd have been much better served in a police officer awareness class.

And, as with the previous police notice, all this information arrived at my parents' home. It was particularly bad timing because I had made some morally inappropriate charges on my parents' credit card that same month. Things were not going well in the Rulli household.

It was a repeat of the conversation I had with my parents after getting busted with the fake ID, except my dad swore even more. He summed it up pretty well. "You've got to stop this s—t."

I felt bad that I had hurt them and once again disappointed them. They loved me, even when I wasn't feeling particularly lovable.

I call God "Father" because Jesus repeatedly called Him Father and taught His apostles to do so. But when I think of my loving Father, it's actually the relationship with my mom that comes to mind. She has a love that forgives, a love that saw the good in an overweight eighteen-year-old kid with a mullet, a growing criminal record, and the inability to hang onto a 3.0 GPA at a pretty expensive Catholic university.

When I think of God as a loving parent, that's when I realize what a jerk I can be. And what a disappointment. And how sorry I really am. So I get up, shake the dust off, and try again.

What's scary about my life is that if I had to do it all over again, I'd probably make the same mistakes. Because Jimmy and Will were a lot of fun, even if it did earn me a permanent record.

5

Adventures in Confession: Part One

I don't remember my First Communion. There is, however, a picture of me and all my classmates in church about to receive First Communion, so I know it happened.

I don't remember my first confession, either, and there's no photographic evidence to prove it happened. I suppose it makes sense that no one took a picture of that event. Something tells me I wouldn't have been smiling.

"OK, Lino," I can imagine my parents saying, "smile at the camera before going and telling that priest all the bad things you've done! We'll be right outside this door waiting for you."

* * *

The next time I went to confession, I was eighteen years old. It's not that I was avoiding the sacrament (although I had plenty of reason to *want* to avoid it). It's just that as far as I recall, no one asked if I wanted to go. Growing up, I don't remember hearing about it when I went to church on Sundays. I went to a Catholic high school, and I don't think it ever came up.

My freshman year of college, I decided to try and get more involved with religion. I went to a lenten service where confession was offered

—considering my teen years were not a model of piety and holiness, I figured I was overdue. I didn't remember what to say or how it worked, but I'd seen it in TV and film and that would have to do.

At my college, though, they didn't have a confessional. No kneeler. No screen to shield me. Nothing like in the movies. We had something called a "Reconciliation Room" where you could more casually confess your sins.

I opened the door of the room and saw a guy sitting at the far end of the space. He wasn't sitting on the floor, but he wasn't sitting in a chair. At first I thought he was on a blanket. As I drew nearer, I realized it was a beanbag chair. There was another one next to him. The equivalent of kneelers, I guess. Classy.

The only light in the room was a candle flickering in a far corner. Enya music was playing from a boom box. Closing the door behind me, I wondered how badly I wanted God's forgiveness. This was asking a lot, especially if I was supposed to go through it with a straight face.

The distance from door to beanbag was perhaps only fifteen feet, but it felt more like thirty. Every step was a step toward awkwardness...I mean a step toward God's mercy.

I sat down on the beanbag, ready to say, "Bless me, Father, for I have sinned"—the only thing I knew about confession—but I wondered if that was appropriate. In this setting, I felt I was the one being sinned against.

The man in the beanbag broke the silence.

"Welcome," he said, like a guy a little too happy to hear my deep, dark secrets.

"I'm Bill. And you are?"

Confused. Angry. Not wanting to share with you. I was so many things.

"I'm Lino," I offered, immediately regretting giving my real name. "You're a priest, right Bill?"

"Yes, yes," he said, trying to convince and reassure both of us.

The only way to get through this was by treating it like a Band-Aid. Let's just rip the sucker off and start listing sins.

After about thirty minutes, we'd both had enough. It was like a heavy-weight fight. I was exhausted. He seemed relieved it was over. We even debated if some of them were sins. He was saying no, I was saying yes. I felt like saying "Hey, it's my confession. Let me confess!"

On the positive side, he wasn't judgmental, that's for sure. He absolved me, thanked me for coming, and that was about it.

It was a relief and I felt good, but it wasn't something I wanted to do on a regular basis.

* * *

Fast-forward seven years, and I'm at St. Peter's Basilica. Lent was approaching, and I thought it'd be nice to go to confession, having sufficiently recovered from the last experience.

I knew St. Peter's would have good, old-fashioned kneelers. To my knowledge, the basilica has no reconciliation room and a strict policy against playing Enya music.

The confessionals are old. So was the priest who heard my sins.

As I knelt behind the screen and tried to get comfortable (something I would not be able to do, literally or spiritually), the priest wasn't as inviting as Bill.

"Yes?"

Uh-oh. This guy's impatient.

"Bless me, Father, for I have sinned. It's been seven years since my last confession."

"Go ahead," he replied curtly. He obviously didn't realize that was *still* the only line I remembered from the movies.

I gave him a laundry list of the seven deadly sins. The strange thing was he wanted the number of times each sin was committed. Truth was, I couldn't remember. So we moved on.

My next batch of sins was about missing Mass and holy days of obligation.

You can probably guess his question: "How many times did you miss Mass?" And you can probably also guess I didn't have an answer.

This guy was a real stickler for rules. And numbers. I thought he was taking this all too seriously. Turns out, he was taking Catholicism seriously. This is what confession involves—when possible, you list the number of times a mortal sin was committed. The idea is if I killed one person, that's a problem. If I killed forty-eight, that's a *real* problem. The priest helps me see which sins are more prevalent so that the squeaky wheel gets the grease.

The priest seemed frustrated that I couldn't even give him a ballpark number of times I'd missed Mass. In retrospect, I get his point: If I'm really sorry, I could have at least tried to figure out how many times I didn't go. Makes me seem a bit more sincere.

Up to this point in my life, I'd pretty much treated religion the same way I treated other things I learned growing up. Dentists want me to floss my teeth. Cops want me to drive the speed limit. Priests want me to go to church every Sunday. That's honestly the way I'd always looked at it.

But back to the priest in Rome. We had come to loggerheads. He wanted numbers. I couldn't do it. He wanted to see more contrition on my part; I thought he was just being crotchety. He could have been a little more understanding, since he was clearly not dealing with a well-formed Catholic. But he'd probably worked in the Vatican for decades and was out of touch with the idea that an adult Catholic had no idea how to go to confession.

These were my first two adult experiences of confession. I'm surprised I returned at all, but I've returned over and over because I sin over and over. To be honest, I'd rather not ever go to confession again. But that would mean I'm done with sinning. So in other words, I'll be going to confession until I die.

6

To None of the Girls I've Loved Before

I'm almost forty years old. Have I ever been married? No.

Engaged? Nope.

Fear of commitment? Yep.

I can barely say the word *commitment* without hyperventilating.

I like to believe that my fear of commitment is a very healthy thing. Christian marriage is not something to be taken lightly. It's the "cord of three" that won't be broken: husband, wife, and God. That's in the Bible if you don't believe me.

So, "till death do me part"? So far, I've been afraid to make that commitment—I'd have to be sick or really, really old. Maybe I'll get married at ninety-one. My ring bearer will be eighty-eight. My wife, twenty-two.

Lots of people make this commitment haphazardly because they don't have the fear of commitment that I have. That's why my attitude is so healthy. At least that's what I keep telling myself.

Since I have a fear of commitment in relationships with women, it's not surprising that I also have a fear of commitment in my relationship with God.

I try to remember, however, that God has made the commitment to us. When Christ went to the cross that was the ultimate commitment of love. He proved his commitment, and is really the model of commitment.

Me? I'm more likely to *be* committed than be *committed.*

Here are a few examples of reasons I have broken up with women, thanks to my fear of commitment. Neurotic reasoning included.

Too Nice

She was perhaps the most beautiful, sweetest, kindest human being I'd ever met. She was absolutely forgiving. Caring. She looked like a model, she helped special needs children for a living, and I, in my brokenness, didn't think I was good enough for her.

I couldn't spend my life with someone that kind and who was in such a good mood all the time. I broke up with her at lunch over a cup of soup. She needed someone much better than me.

Small Teeth

To be fair, her entire head was small. When I went to kiss her, it was as if I were kissing a shrunken head. Her teeth were like Chiclets. My friends told me that I was crazy, that they were proportionate to the rest of her body. Fine. Does it make it any better to say her legs were too small? No. So it was her teeth, OK? I didn't know at what point in the relationship I could bring up getting teeth enlargement.

As an aside, I don't want a woman with big teeth, because watching those choppers dive into a sandwich could be disturbing—like seeing a beaver gnawing on wood.

Lack of Control in Movie Theaters

I liked this girl a lot until we saw a horror film and she freaked out.

First, the movie was her choice. I wasn't forcing her to go to a scary movie. Second, you know that buildup before the guy jumps out of the closet and kills everyone? The music is building, the character about to be killed is looking around cautiously—well, this girl screams seconds before anything happens. She's a premature screamer. And while that may have its advantages in my personal life, she spooked everyone in the theater. She'd scream, everyone around us would scream, and then the actual scary part would happen. It was bad manners.

Too Athletic

I met this girl at a bar. The first thing she commented on were my Adidas soccer shoes. This should have been the first sign of trouble. She was in a volleyball league Tuesdays and Thursdays. She went mountain-biking three times a week. She swam a few laps at the gym every morning. Enough. I get it. You're athletic. Your apartment smells like a locker room. Great.

Foodie

This girl loved food too much. No, this isn't a reference to her weight. It's just that she was more interested in what was on the plate than what was on my mind. We had more photos of the food we ate than of the two of us. "How was your day?" would turn into a menu of the day. And not just an "I had a cheeseburger and fries" would do. Oh, no. What type of meat? How was it prepared? What were the condiments? Sea-salt fries? Wedge fries? Skin on? I was dating Rachael Ray without the success.

By the way, why do they get to be called foodies? Groupies aren't fans of groups. Moonies aren't fans of the moon. But foodies get to declare they are more into food than the rest of us.

Too White

I love the sun. Few things put me in a better mood than being outside in the sun. Doesn't have to be a beach setting, but I'm a bit of a tan-a-holic. This girl, though, was pale white. Dan Brown could have modeled his albino monk character on her. Eight seconds in the sun and she was red as Bill Clinton after a good laugh. I couldn't handle it. We couldn't go to the beach, we couldn't lay out on the grass in Central Park, we could barely go outside. I was dating a vampire before vampires were cool.

Non-Photogenic Girl

If I'd dated her before the age of digital technology, I could have let this slide. Unfortunately, I dated her in the age of Facebook and cell phone cameras. It was a long distance relationship, the only images of her were unflattering, and I couldn't handle it. I spent more time with her image than I did with her in real life. Oh, and she was beautiful in real life—just couldn't take a photo to save herself. The long distance part was hard enough, but I couldn't imagine our life together. Ugly photo from our wedding day on the wall. Weird-looking honeymoon photos. She never looked happy. More like she had just sucked on something really tart.

Smelled like Garlic

This was a relationship I really messed up. She was gorgeous, lots of fun, sang in the church choir, and always had a positive energy. We went out to an Italian restaurant for dinner one night, and she ate something with lots of garlic in it. When I went to kiss her good night, the smell was overwhelming.

The next day, I started to call her, but I recalled how garlicky her breath was. I couldn't ask her out again because I couldn't get the thought of her breath out of my mind. I really couldn't get over it. To this day, when I think of her, I mostly think of garlic.

Big Nose

In perhaps the irony of all ironies, I once quit dating a girl because her nose was too big. I met her online, we went out on some very fun dates, but, damn, she had a big nose. I never admitted it until now, but I was afraid any kids we would have together would be circus freaks. The poor kids would be all nose.

* * *

I could go on and on.

God gives me free will, but when it involves my dating life, I really wish He wouldn't. When it comes to dating, I can't be trusted to do anything other than say, "No, thanks."

. . . . 7

Brother Lino

There was a time in my life when I really wanted to serve others. I was passionate about wanting to serve in a foreign country. Be a missionary. Evangelize in faraway lands. Thankfully, those desires faded—since those career choices typically don't pay very well.

One Christmas Eve I was doing some last-minute shopping—aka beginning my Christmas shopping—and bumped into Terry, a friend from my college days.

"So, Terry," I said, "other than presumably just starting your Christmas shopping as well, what are you up to nowadays?" Terry and I were friends in the days before Facebook—when you didn't know every detail about the life of any person who's crossed your path.

"I'm just home for Christmas break," he replied, implying I knew where he was back from.

He was tan, so I figured somewhere warm, but I wasn't in the mood to guess. I had presents to frantically purchase, creating the illusion I cared about those I love.

"I'm living in Nassau, Bahamas, teaching high-school religion." Score. Maybe that's what I could do, too.

What a sacrifice this would be. Teaching in the Bahamas! What a soldier for Christ I'd become. What I wouldn't give up in service to the Lord.

I got Terry's phone number in Nassau and said I'd call him in a few weeks to learn more.

I moved to the Bahamas in 1996 to teach high-school religion. Would that have happened if I hadn't bumped into Terry? Hard to imagine. Had I gone Christmas shopping at some point other than 6:30 PM on Christmas Eve, would I have moved to the Bahamas? I doubt it.

Sure, God, being God, could have gotten me there some other way, but it's these little coincidences in life that have me thanking God—and that drive me crazy at the same time.

I try to constantly be aware of where God might be leading me, which drives me absolutely bonkers. Should I go here for lunch, or there for lunch? Who might I see? What might God have in store for me? I trust in God's plan, but I'm always afraid I'm going to screw it up. Faith and a neurotic personality don't always mix well.

* * *

Teaching in the Bahamas sounded like the greatest gig in the world. I pictured the school as a little straw hut on the beach. The kids would be wearing leis—for some reason, they were Hawaiian in my mind's eye—coconuts in hand, and when they weren't busy making Mr. Rulli another mai tai, they were enthralled with my beautiful explanations of the faith.

Turned out to be a little different than that. For starters, the neighborhood I lived in was called Fox Hill, perhaps because you had to be quick like a fox to get out with your life. To say it was prone to crime is to say Larry King is prone to marriage.

Toward the end of my first year there, I was talking to a guy living in the neighborhood. "You been mugged yet?" he asked. I said, "No," and thought to myself: *And I hope that trend continues.*

"You've gotta be kidding. You've lived in the neighborhood an entire year and not once? Not a gun pulled on you? Nothing?" He then called to some of his buddies, the guys you see standing around on a corner, up to no good.

"Hey, get over here," he yelled to his friends, adding that I had never been robbed.

"You ain't ever been robbed, eh?" his friend asked inquisitively. At this point I assumed they were going to do the honors. They looked at me as an oddity. They debated among themselves, as if I weren't there, why that could be.

"Maybe he don't look like he got a wallet on him," one guy said. "You're more likely to have to give him some money versus stealing from him."

Another guy had his own theory: "He kinda looks crazy, like he's gonna pull out a cutlass if you say the wrong thing."

All this talk started to make me angry. I was almost hurt I hadn't been mugged. No one thought I was worth their time to mug? They didn't think I had anything to steal? Regardless, I was thankful my "mugless" streak continued.

* * *

I had chosen this neighborhood because there was a Benedictine monastery attached to the school, and I was considering becoming a monk. During my last few months in the Bahamas, I lived in the monastery and really enjoyed my time there. Many mornings, I would wake up in time for morning prayer. After class, I would try to make it to daily Mass or evening prayer.

I liked the rhythm of monastic life. I liked the structure of prayer and work. I really liked being a part of a community that prayed together, ate together, drank together. It was like a clean frat house.

My room was just a cell with a bed, a desk, and a chair. I loved the fact that it was so simple—it let me focus on reading, praying, preparing lessons, or whatever. Many nights I laughed at how strange and contradictory a person I had become: I loved hanging out with my friends, meeting girls on the beach, going out for nice meals, having drinks. At the same time, I enjoyed the quiet and peace of the monastic life.

The monastery had a little television room where I would usually go at the end of the evening to watch some TV and relax. One of the older monks, a priest in his late seventies, was a tall, lanky guy with long white hair and big muttonchop sideburns. He looked like a skinnier version of fifteenth-century frescoes of God the Father in some European church. He talked slowly, he walked slowly, he always had a smile on his face, and he was one of the most peaceful men I'd ever met.

Every night he'd come into the TV room and head to the adjacent kitchen area. He'd take a glass, drop in some ice cubes, pour in his nightly Scotch, and watch whatever I was watching. Didn't matter if he came in halfway through an episode of *Seinfeld*. He just wanted to have a drink and watch some TV.

It was his nightly routine, so after a few weeks of living there, I had to ask: "Father, does the Scotch help you go to sleep?"

He paused, smiled a little bigger, and said, "Don't know. Never tried going to sleep without it." And with that, he laughed, finished his drink, and shuffled down the long corridor to his cell for the night.

Near the end of my time there, I went to the prior, Father Benedict, to talk about the possibility of becoming a monk.

"What do you think, Father, should I become Brother Lino?"

"No," he said, with the assurance of someone who didn't have to think twice.

Well, that was easy.

"You're too immature," he continued, making it sound more like a breakup than vocational discernment. "You're twenty-four and there's plenty you still want to do with your life. If you joined the monastery now, you'd be here for a few years, get restless, want to try other things, and you'd leave. So, no, I've told the abbot that I don't think you should be a monk."

"But," I argued, "maybe that's just because I'm a restless guy. Didn't St. Augustine say 'Our hearts are restless until they rest in you, O Lord'?"

Father Benedict thought for a moment and said, "Yes, Augustine did say that."

And with that, I wasn't joining the monastery. It was no longer only single women and muggers who were rejecting me; a bunch of celibate guys were now on record for rejecting me.

That hurts.

* * *

I learned I wouldn't become a monk on a Saturday afternoon. A sunny day in the Bahamas, so I went to the beach. Could be worse.

I headed to Paradise Island, picked my regular spot on the sand, and put my towel down. There was a couple sitting about twenty-five yards away—white Bahamians, both in their mid-thirties.

"Wanna beer?" the guy asked.

"Sure, thanks," I said, walking over to my new friends.

We had a beer and some small talk.

As we opened our second beers, he offered some pot. Though I'm always uncomfortable saying no to anyone, perhaps the monks saying "no" to me earlier in the day gave me some confidence. I passed on the grass.

"So what do you do for a living?" he asked, assuming there must be a reason I was saying no to an illegal substance.

"Teach high-school religion," I replied.

"You know I don't have a problem with Christianity...," he responded. Uh-oh. When someone tells me they don't have a problem with Christianity, it means they're going to tell me the *problems* they have with the faith. Same goes for the person who says, "We have to talk." That really means, "I have to talk. You have to listen."

The thought occurred to me: Cut him off at the pass. "So you don't have a problem with Christianity?" I said as quickly as I could. "Me either!"

"Well," he continued, "I think the Bible got a few things wrong."

"Like what?" I asked innocently enough.

"Well, it's my belief that when Jesus was born the wise men weren't following a star in the sky. It was actually an alien spacecraft."

Damn, that must be some strong weed. "Is that the pot talking?" I asked.

"No, man. I think it makes the most sense. The aliens led the three wise men to the manger. It doesn't work for them to follow a star during the daytime, so what would be guiding them? And as the stars move in the night sky, the wise men would get lost. But a spacecraft could be something they followed day and night till they reached their destination."

OK. Fair enough. So Snoop Dogg's dealer here had no problem with God becoming man. No issues with the Virgin giving birth. The real sticking point of the nativity story for Willie Nelson's brother was that it wasn't a star. It was a spacecraft filled with aliens.

"Look, I don't want to just be a big apologist for Catholicism here," I started in, "but let me say why I don't believe aliens were at Jesus' birth..."

He looked pleased, and a little surprised, that I was taking this conversation seriously.

"First, aliens aren't polite. I have yet to hear of a single alien experience that goes well. They're usually not guiding wise men. They're usually abducting and probing. And since most alien stories deal with that type of boorish behavior, it means aliens would have probed the wise men. And I can't sign off on the idea that Gaspar, Melchior, and Balthasar were poked and prodded."

"Well," he replied, "you're just saying that because, if aliens exist, it changes everything you believe in."

"No," I argued back, "the existence of aliens has nothing to do with Christianity. If aliens *did* exist, it wouldn't change one thing about faith. The story of salvation history is salvation for humanity; it says nothing about Jesus dying on the cross for the sins of aliens. Doesn't change a thing."

"Huh," he said with a shrug, "guess you have a point." With that, we cracked open another beer and changed topics.

Apparently, even though I wasn't a monk, God could still use me to spread the gospel. Or else my new friend was just too buzzed to stay focused.

* * *

In 2009, I was in Nassau for vacation and went to Sunday Mass at a parish not far from Paradise Island. To my surprise, the celebrant was Father Benedict. I was practically smiling the entire Mass, thinking about the part he played in my life and the guidance he gave me.

He was right. I hadn't been ready to become a monk, and I was grateful he had been honest with me.

As Mass wound down, I couldn't wait for his reaction on seeing me again. In my mind, I was reorganizing my calendar for the day: He'd want to hang out, eat, maybe encourage me to renew my discernment to the religious life.

After Mass, I went up and said hello.

"Hey, Father, how are you?" I said, with both arms open, assuming he'd want to embrace this prodigal son.

He extended his hand for a handshake. "Good, how are you?"

You could tell he recognized me but wasn't sure from where. Had I stolen his hubcaps? Was I a student from long ago? Someone whose vocation he determined in between bites of a sandwich?

"Lino Rulli," I said, unsure of my own name at this point. "I lived here about ten years ago..."

He cut me off. "Oh, yes, Lino, how are you?" I believe he did remember me at this point, and we had a little chat about life, how things were going, and that was it.

Two minutes later we said good-bye. And as I walked away from the church, I thought to myself: "I wonder if I should have discerned my vocation to the religious life a little better. And maybe I should have tried some of that weed."

8

Mom

Every night, at 9:55 PM Central Standard Time, I call my mom.

"Hello, hello," she answers.

"Hello, just me," I say.

"And how's Lino this evening?" For some reason, this is the one and only time she refers to me in the third person. It's as if I'm Lino's assistant calling in.

"He's fine, how are you?" I respond.

"I'm fine, fine," is her nightly response. Mom likes repeating words, as you can tell, tell.

For several minutes, I'm regaled by stories of retirement. Some days she and her friends play music for, as she calls them, "the little old people" at the nursing home. Other days she's out shopping for things she'll return the next week. "I didn't do anything today" is the one that particularly stings. Man, I'd love to do nothing.

Our nightly phone call isn't really for her to give me her daily updates, though. And it's not for me to give her my daily updates, either. It's all a front for the underlying message: To make sure I'm still alive.

"OK, well, I'm happy to hear things are going well," she inevitably answers.

I never said things were going well, by the way. It just happens I wasn't abducted and tortured. That's my mom's definition of things going well.

I guess it's a glass-half-full approach to life, but I don't wake up every day thinking, "Hope today isn't the day I'm chained to some dude's radiator, begging for food…"

"Well, I love you very much and have a good night's sleep," she ends the call.

"I love you too," I respond, knowing she'll sleep well.

And with that, our nightly tradition is over.

* * *

Mom is a retired high-school French teacher. She had two goals for me in my childhood: to teach me French and to teach me the faith.

Early on, she realized I was a failure on the religion front. "Lino," she once asked me in front of the class—she taught my religious education classes—"who was the first pope?"

"Moses," I answered. Not only was I wrong, I didn't even have the right testament. (For all you trivia buffs out there, the correct answer is Saint Peter.)

As for my French, I don't speak fluently but I can get around France. Take, for example, this sentence:

"Je m'appelle Lino et je voudrais jambon," which translates, "My name is Lino and I would like ham." What more do I need to know? Names and meat products; that's all I need to get around in a foreign land.

Oh, and I know one other phrase: "Je me rends" which means "I surrender." This seems to be a common phrase for the French.

Granted, this is not a very impressive mastery of the language considering my mom's been teaching me since I was a little kid. Most summer days consisted of Mom inviting the neighbor kids and me to the garage for French lessons. I never understood why we didn't meet in the living room, or the unfinished basement, or the kitchen. The garage was a pleasant enough atmosphere, I guess: oil stains, broken glass that lodged in your flip-flops, and the general feeling that you'd rather be anywhere on a warm June day than in your parent's garage/classroom.

Mom forced me into these classes, of course. I wasn't a fourth-grader who longed for school so much that he wanted to conjugate French verbs in his free time. I was never clear about how she got the neighbor kids to show up.

* * *

My mom and I are alike in so many ways. We look alike. We have the same interests. And we both annoy the hell out of me.

But my mom is the greatest human being I know. I say that not because it shows a soft side to me, or may increase my chances to get dates, but because I honestly think it's true.

She's the first person I pray for every morning and the last person I pray for every night. Mom is the first and foremost person in my life.

The thing that bugs me about my mom is that she's apparently holy without effort. Prayers come easily to her. Faith comes easily to her. Virtues come easily to her.

When I was growing up, my parents and I took an annual family vacation. As I got older and made my own money, I wanted to start treating them to family vacations. But knowing the stress that came when the three of us traveled together, I started doing our family trips without the whole family: Mom and I would go on a family vacation. Then, Pops and I would go on a family vacation.

I gave each of them vouchers entitled "Travel with Lino" to wherever they wanted to go in the continental United States and Puerto Rico. I'd cover flights and hotels; they were on their own for meals and drinks.

Mom chose San Diego in February. The city that was supposed to be sunny and warm year round was cold and miserable. When we checked into the Holiday Inn (hey, I said I'd pay, I didn't say it was the Four Seasons) even the receptionist apologized for the weather. "Welcome to San Diego. Bad timing." Something like bad weather on vacation can really bum me out. I wonder if God has it out for me. Mom, on the other hand, is always at peace. "Oh, well," she said, "sometimes the weather is bad."

We had a nice meal on our first night and then watched some TV in her room. As she was preparing for bed, and I was about to leave for my own room, she mentioned that she says the same prayer every night before going to sleep, a prayer she learned as a little kid. It goes:

Oh, Jesus dear, before I sleep I thank thee and I pray
That thou wouldst take away my sins committed through this day
I believe in thee, I hope in thee, I love thee with all my heart.
Bless thou my body, soul, and friends, my Lord, my God, thou art.
Oh, Mary Mother, virgin dear, St. Joseph, guardian blest,
My angel and my patron saints, care for me while I rest.

See, I remember virtually nothing more from my childhood prayers than the Our Father and Hail Mary. But Mom can rattle this off with ease.

I assume Mom got her faith from her father, Gino Andreassi, who died just before I was born. Mom was pregnant with me at the time, and it breaks my heart to think he never got a chance to meet me.

* * *

Angelo Gino Armando Rulli is my legal name.

Angelo is my given name, but I've gone by Lino since Day One because my dad's name is Angelo as well. They could have called me Angelino, which means Little Angel. That's right, I'm a little angel by definition. But then my mom and dad shortened that to Lino, which means *little*. Which means I've been insecure since Day One.

Gino Armando, my middle names, are in honor of my maternal grandfather, Gino, and my paternal grandfather, Armando. I'm talking about Gino now. Armando will have to wait till I write my second book.

From all accounts, Gino Andreassi was a real man's man. He grew up in Villa San Angelo, a little town in the Abruzzo region of Italy, about a two-hour drive from Rome. It's a picturesque area with rolling hills, rivers, waterfalls, and one of the tallest mountains in Italy, Gran Sasso. Gino was born in the family home, as was his father before him, and his father before him. In other words, it's literally a family home, and we still own it.

Though only 5'7", Gino was strong like bull. He and his two brothers, Achille and Giambattista, fought for the Italian army in World War I. Gino carried the heavy part of the cannon as an Alpine soldier. He and his brothers corresponded during the war with their mother, always expressing love and devotion to family and God.

After the Great War, Gino returned home and then joined his brothers in the States. He worked in New York, on the Hudson Tunnel, as a hot-rivet man. He then worked in the limestone mines of Pennsylvania. Tough jobs for a tough man.

While in Pennsylvania, he noticed that Ricardo, a guy from his hometown who also worked in the mines, was corresponding with a certain Josephine. Gino and Josephine had known each other since childhood but had never dated. Well, now Gino was interested. And he began intercepting and stealing the letters Josephine sent to Ricardo.

Ricardo wondered why Josephine stopped writing him. "Is she seeing someone new?" he would ask Gino. "Does she not care for me anymore?" Likewise, Josephine wondered why Ricardo no longer replied to her letters. The two eventually broke up.

In 1926 Gino returned to Villa and started dating Josephine. When Ricardo heard the whole story, he showed up and confronted Gino for what he did.

Ricardo pulled out a gun and shot Gino in the leg. Freaked out, Ricardo then jumped on his motorcycle and was never seen again.

That's love. My grandfather took a bullet for my grandmother.

Gino was always devoted to Our Lady. When he and Josephine married, they honeymooned in Pompeii—to visit the shrine of Our Lady of Pompeii. Some would think going to church on a honeymoon isn't all that romantic, but I wouldn't argue with Gino.

And that devotion to Mary continued throughout his life.

One day, when he was working at a bar, he went into the walk-in cooler for the beer kegs. The door closed behind him and he was trapped. The temperature was below freezing and he knew he couldn't last long. He pounded on the door, but no one came to rescue him. He asked the Virgin Mary to intercede for him. If he survived, he promised to continue his devotion to Our Lady of Pompeii and contribute greatly to the shrine.

Hours later, help arrived and Gino survived. Unlike me, his squirrely grandson, my grandfather was not the type to welsh on a deal with God. See, when I make deals with God I usually find a loophole, but not Gino.

I took a trip to the shrine of Our Lady of Pompeii a few years ago to pray for the repose of the souls of my grandparents and to thank Mary for her intercession. All around the church, attached to the walls, were silver "ornaments" (for lack of a better word). A silver leg here, a silver tongue there. It was like being in an anatomy class where the body parts were made of silver.

They were placed there by those who were healed as proof that their prayers were answered. Each *ex voto,* as these offerings are known, are an expression of gratitude for an answered prayer. For example, let's say I lose my voice. I ask the intercession of the Virgin Mary—or, more specifically in this case, Our Lady of Pompeii—on my behalf. If my voice returns, I would buy an ex voto to place on the wall in thanks for the answered prayer and also to encourage others to believe that prayers really do get answered.

There was no silver walk-in beer cooler ornament on the wall. I'm sure my grandfather would have wanted to purchase one, but those aren't exactly standard ex voto fare.

Visiting that church connected me to my grandparents in a very cool way. The Italian American kid visiting his homeland to honor his grandparents. See, some days I seem like a pretty good person.

* * *

The story of how Gino, Josephine, and their kids came to America is the stuff of legend, but my aunt swears it's true.

When he was fifteen, my great-uncle Mike worked on the farm in the Abruzzo hills tending cows, goats, and sheep. One day, Uncle Mike was herding the cows back toward home. He gave one cow a push in the wrong direction, and either Mike was the strongest guy on earth or owned the clumsiest cow on earth, but either way the cow rolled off the hill, fell into a waterfall, and died.

I like to take credit for my family inventing cow-tipping, but there's no proof of that.

When Mike returned home, his father yelled at him. And by "yelled at him," I mean "beat him."

The next day, Mike ran away from home. A few days later, he heard that someone from town was leaving for Canada, and Mike asked if he could tag along. They hitched a ride to Le Havre, France, and from there caught a ship. He had no papers, so he had to sneak on board. Eventually he arrived in Manitoba. Illegally.

He found a job digging ditches, which apparently was better than tending unbalanced cows in Italy. One day at work he stepped on a nail. As he hobbled down the road looking for medical assistance, he met a married couple—also from Italy—who helped him. They thought medical treatment in the States was the best option, however, so they put him in the trunk of their car and crossed the border into Minnesota. Illegally.

His foot healed, Uncle Mike headed down to the state capital, St. Paul, looking for work. He made friends with some fellow Italians, and though no one would say he joined the Mafia, let's just say he didn't *not* join the Mafia. That would be illegal, and he doesn't break laws.

He owned a bar and restaurant in the city for a few years, but was arrested in 1933. Something about reselling cigarettes that had fallen off the back of a truck and some booze that may not have been acquired legally. He was sentenced and sent to Leavenworth penitentiary, but he wasn't a rat. He wouldn't say who he had worked with or how he got his hands on the booze and cigarettes. Years later, after being released from prison, the not-Mafia took care of him financially for the rest of his life.

Before leaving for Leavenworth, however, he needed to find someone to take care of the bar. Someone who had a clean record, wasn't associated with the mob, and could use honest work. He wrote a letter to his sister Josephine, who was still in Villa, to see if her husband, Gino, would be interested in coming to Minnesota and taking over.

The offer to move to Minnesota meant that Gino would have a good job and the family could live upstairs from the restaurant and bar rent-free. So in 1935, Gino, his wife, and two daughters moved to America permanently. Legally.

Four years later, my mom was born. And that's how my mom's family came to America. Thanks to the not-Mafia.

* * *

Gino drank, he smoked, he built stuff, and he took care of his family. He made sure his daughters could take singing and piano lessons from the nuns at the Catholic schools.

One of my favorite photos of him hangs in an Italian restaurant in St. Paul. Amid the pictures of Frank Sinatra and other notable Italians, there's a photo of my grandfather and a group of guys at church. They were members of a group dedicated to the Sacred Heart devotion.

It feels like the faith of a time long gone, and I don't know if there are still men like that anymore. God knows I'm not one. But I carry an image of the Sacred Heart in my wallet, to remind me how weak I am compared to Gino. And though I don't have the devotion to the Virgin Mary that I should, I'm devoted to the most virtuous woman I know: my mom. And that's a start.

9

Stargazing

Whenever I visit a foreign country, I feel bad for their celebrities. Celebrities in foreign lands fall into three categories:

1. They have our celebrities, like Brad Pitt, Angelina Jolie, and George Clooney.
2. They also have our celebrities who are bigger in their country than in our own, like David Hasselhoff.
3. They have *their* celebrities.

Their celebrities are on the cover of gossip magazines and television shows. They look and act like celebrities, but because I don't live in their country I have no idea who they are. I pity them.

It must be a real blow to the ego when you can cross a border and people no longer know who you are. At that point, I'm not even sure the term *celebrity* fits. If you're huge in France but can visit Greece without being bothered, it's like you're the popular guy at work or school. You're only popular within particular boundaries.

When *our* celebrities travel overseas, everyone knows them. When *their* celebrities come to us, they have to explain who, exactly, they are.

He might say, "I'm like the Charles Nelson Reilly of Portugal!"

Or she might argue, "I'm the Charo of Ukraine!" We have to take their word for it.

But whether I know them or not, I love me some celebrity.

* * *

In the spring of 1993, five of my college friends and I drove from Minnesota to Daytona Beach for spring break.

At a bar one night, one of my friends looked around, pointed and said: "Hey, that's the Red Rocker. That's Sammy Hagar!"

Sammy was the lead singer of Van Halen. He'd replaced David Lee Roth a few years earlier. Personally, I was a Roth fan, but the weird thing about celebrity is that even if you don't like the person, you still have to care. It's un-American not to.

The only problem was that we weren't sure it was really Sammy Hagar. The guy had the long, curly blonde hair, but he looked kind of pudgy. Too heavy to be a rock star.

There was only one way to find out. Some drunken college kid would have to yell something out to him. "David Lee Roth was way better in Van Halen," I bellowed across the bar. "Roth Rules!"

To which the man replied, "I agree."

OK, it's Sammy Hagar. No doubt about it. He's had drunk college kids saying that to him for years. To make sure, however, my friend Todd went over to Sammy and his date.

"Listen," Todd said, "everyone wants to know if you're Sammy Hagar or not. Just be honest with me, are you? If you're not, I'll tell everyone to leave you alone, and if you are, I'll still tell everyone to leave you alone, but at least I'll know. It'll be our little secret."

Surprisingly, Sammy wasn't interested in sharing little secrets with a complete stranger. Todd made it clear he wasn't leaving until he got an answer—so Sammy and his date left.

Sammy's half-drunk glass of beer was still on the table, and Todd brought it back to us. "Look, guys, it's Sammy Hagar's beer! Pass it around and take a sip! We're rock stars!"

When the glass came to me, I thought to myself: "Great. All the health risks of a rock star's lifestyle without any of the benefits."

We ended up stealing the glass from the bar so that we could tell people for years to come: "Sammy Hagar drank from this glass. We're pretty sure it was Sammy. Well, we were drunk, but for sure a heavy guy with long, curly blonde hair drank from this glass."

* * *

When I see a celebrity, I want what they have: attention, notoriety, money, annoying college kids approaching me. But as a Catholic, I know I'm supposed to be striving for saintliness...not celebrity. Problem is, when I look at paintings of saints, I think: "Wow. That's not me."

A celebrity's life? I get it. A saint's life? I'm not sure.

Technically, the saints are our celebrities, even though we don't call them that. They're folks in heaven who lived heroic lives of virtue, and they're the ones I should try to imitate.

But I feel this pull, or contradiction, in the things that interest me. For example, I'm as interested in seeing the chalice that St. Philip Neri drank from at Mass as I am in seeing Sammy Hagar's glass. I want to be more interested in Church stuff and less interested in pop-culture stuff, but the holy stuff seems fleeting because I'm so into the stuff on earth.

It seems way easier to be a celebrity, too. A few good auditions, a couple of lucky breaks—if it can happen to Carrot Top, it can happen to me. And with the advent of reality TV, all you need to become a celebrity is a willingness to lose some weight, your temper, or your clothes.

Mother Teresa once said that in order to be a saint you have to seriously want to be one. So I try, feebly, to be a saint. Frankly, the sinner in me doesn't think it sounds like much fun.

* * *

I saw a lot of celebrities when I lived in the Bahamas, often at the Atlantis casino on Paradise Island where all the tourists—and celebrities—go. Some friends and I were at the casino one night when we noticed a crowd gathering in the high-rollers' section. I walked over to see who was drawing all the attention.

It was O.J. Simpson.

He was in the high-roller, double-murderer (alleged) section, and people gathered around to watch him gamble. I'm always a fan of groups of people jammed tightly together for a common cause, so I joined the fray.

I said out loud, to no one in particular, what came immediately to mind. "He's got a huge head! Anyone else think he's got an enormous cranium?" There was some murmuring and agreement in the crowd.

One guy proclaimed, "Yeah, it's the size of three normal human heads!"

Another said, "You could throw a movie on his forehead and it'd be a drive-in theater." Again, hyperbole, but a huge head.

A lady to my left jumped in: "What is he even doing here? Shouldn't he be in jail?"

"The glove didn't fit," I reminded her. "They had no choice but to acquit."

At about that time, O.J. looked up at the crowd. There were fifty or sixty of us in pretty tight quarters, but he didn't scan the crowd; he looked directly at me and no one else. We stared at each other. I didn't blink. I thought to myself, "I hope he doesn't kill me (allegedly)."

It felt like minutes, though it was probably more like ten seconds. The people around me were uncomfortable. Why was The Juice staring at me? Finally I smiled, waved, and mouthed the words, "Hi, O.J."

He smiled, waved, and went back to gambling.

"What was that?" the woman next to me asked.

"I have no idea," I responded. "Why *did* O.J. just say hello to me?"

Another guy said, "Why he said hello is completely irrelevant compared to the fact that he murdered two people."

"Allegedly!" we all said in unison.

Eventually my friends and I went to the bar, had a drink, and they called it a night. I stayed for my weekly tradition: smoking a Cuban cigar (they're legal in the Bahamas) while walking around the grounds.

Between the casino and the beach, the Atlantis has a beautiful outdoor area with palm trees, pools, fountains, and aquariums. There are several big buildings and smaller villas, and though it's not well lit, I've always felt safe there.

As I was walking down the path, I heard rattling near one of the bushes, and who should come walking out? O.J. I have no idea what he was doing there.

He seemed startled to see me. "Hey, uh, hey, man, how you doing?" he asked. I don't know if he recognized me from the casino or not.

"Doing good. Just out having a cigar," I responded.

"Uhh…" He paused and looked around like he was waiting for someone or something. "Oh, yeah?" he asked. "What are you smoking?" I could see he didn't care about the question or the answer.

I responded confidently, because it's the same cigar I smoked every week. "A Cohiba Siglo IV. Ever had one?"

"Oh, all right, all right, great, then." He didn't answer my question. Interesting. More silence.

It seemed that neither of us really had a purpose in being where we were. The idea of me walking around smoking a cigar was as random as him coming out of the bushes. I did feel the burden of proof was on him, though.

"OK, well, see ya, O.J.," was all I could think to say.

"Yeah, all right, man."

And I walked away. But I thought it was pretty cool. I had just met another celebrity.

* * *

The Church says we are all called to be saints, but most days it seems like an unattainable goal. A saint's life? I don't know. They don't act or talk like me. I'm not forgiving; I don't want to spread the faith that much. I'm not there yet. Not sure if I ever will be.

In truth, being Christlike is scary.

Feed the hungry? I've helped out at soup kitchens, but I'm really uncomfortable there. I'd rather make a donation to a food pantry by credit card—and collect frequent-flyer miles at the same time.

Visit those in prison? I did prison ministry when I was in graduate school. I never knew what to say when I'd leave. "See you next week. I'm going to go out and, um, be outside doing whatever I want." It was always awkward.

Clothe the naked? Depends on who the naked person is.

I don't want to be last, I want to be first. I want the seat of honor.

In other words, I realize how far away I am from what Christianity is all about.

Saint Lino Rulli? Tough to believe. Celebrity Lino Rulli? Maybe for fifteen minutes.

10

Thai Temptation

I visited Thailand in 2005 with my friend Pat, his wife, and two of her friends. We split our time with a week on the island of Koh Samui, followed by a week in Bangkok.

In Koh Samui, we sampled the local beers, ate the freshest of seafood—and noticed the large number of female prostitutes. At first, it was a shock to the system.

We'd walk down the street and a woman would smile at me and say, "Like a massage, handsome man?"

Being the articulate handsome man I am, I usually came up with a clever response: "Uhh… um… no, sorry."

Day in and day out, at restaurants, bars, and just walking along the street, beautiful women were constantly offering themselves to us. It was uncomfortable, but by the time we'd been there a week, it seemed natural. I was totally acclimated to the idea that prostitution was a normal activity—just not something for me. Strange what a person can get used to.

By the time we got to Bangkok, we needed something new to shock our systems and we found it: a three-story complex that held about seventy-five bars. The concierge at our hotel had recommended it as "a truly Thai experience."

The bars in the middle of the complex were like typical bars in the States. All along the complex, however, were strip clubs. It's free to get in (financially, not necessarily morally). The girls each have a number on them, so, in this land of legal prostitution, you need only say, "I want lucky thirteen." You pay, take the girl home, and that's it.

The five of us were in the bar—not the strip club—section having a few beers and laughs, when an American guy walks by.

"This place is crazy, huh?" he said.

"Yeah, it's really crazy," one of the women in our group replied.

He was from Texas, and his name was John. As we'd find out, this was not an un-ironic name. He was on his own, visiting Thailand for work, and in between small talk we found out we were all staying at the same hotel.

We finished our beers and decided to head back. As we left, John said he wasn't going to the hotel just yet. "I'm going to buy some fruit. I love the fresh fruit in Thailand and this way I'll have a little breakfast ready for tomorrow morning."

"OK, see you at the pool tomorrow," we said, and that was our night.

The next morning Pat and I arrived at the pool at about nine. A few minutes later John showed up, sat down with a towel, and said, "Will you think less of me if I tell you that after I got back to the hotel last night, I went back to the bar, paid twenty-five dollars, and got a girl?"

"Really? How did that come about?" I asked, in my most nonpartisan of voices. The journalist in me demanded answers.

"Well, we got back to the room, and first she took a shower. While she was in there, I hid my wallet and valuables just to make sure she wouldn't steal anything. After she got out of the shower, it was my turn to shower. And then, well…"

Just at that moment, Pat's wife and friends show up at the pool. Guess we'd have to fill in the details on our own.

After a full day at the pool, we all went out for the night and, as we got ready to return to the hotel, John once again said, "I'm gonna stop by the market and get some fruit." Which means he's gonna get a girl. Looking at Pat and me, he went a little further: "Aren't you guys going to?"

We looked at each other. "Um, no thanks."

This pattern continued for several nights.

* * *

The last day of our trip was a Sunday. I woke up that morning and told the group I'd meet them around noon.

I said I wanted to get some shopping done, but in fact I was going to church. For some reason, I'm still not comfortable telling people, "I'm off now to worship the one true God." It's a combination of insecurity and not wanting to condemn others for failing to join me for worship.

Now all I had to do was find a Catholic church. I went to the hotel reception desk to ask where the nearest one might be.

"Sawatdee," I began the conversation, utilizing one of the three words I'd learned in the Thai language. After "hello," however, we went back to English. "I'm looking for a church."

The young female receptionist was eager to help, but unfortunately she was unfamiliar with the word *church*.

"Shirts?" she said with a smile.

"No, church," I repeated.

"Shirts, like pants and shirts?" she asked again, this time pointing to my pants and shirts.

"No, umm, church," I said, this time making the sign of the cross—"like God."

Seeing me touch my forehead, stomach, left shoulder, and right shoulder—apparently for no reason—must have been very confusing for her.

"I'm sorry," she said with a smile. "I don't understand."

She gave me a map of the area and I saw that there was a "shirts" only a ten-minute walk from my hotel. Not only was the church well marked, it even advertised Mass times on the hotel map! Nice work, Catholic Church of Thailand.

The walk to Mass was easy and along busy roads. At an intersection, while waiting for the light to change, a guy handing out pamphlets advertising men's suits asked me how I liked Thailand.

"It's great," I said. "The food is awesome. The beaches are beautiful. Everyone is so nice."

"And the girls?" he asked. "You've been with our women?" He seemed to have such pride in his voice that I didn't want to hurt his feelings by saying no.

"Oh, yes," I said, betraying whatever values and morals I have. "The women are great."

He went on to extol the virtues of the Thai prostitutes a little longer, the light turned green, and we waved good-bye.

And I went to worship…

* * *

Later that night, we all went out for one final dinner. After a huge feast of shrimp, lobster, pad Thai, dessert, some beers—all for the whopping price of eight dollars—Pat's wife and friends went back to the hotel and it was just me, Pat, and The John.

We decided to head for a bar for a few last drinks. It was a normal bar, not a strip club or girlie bar, but this being Bangkok, there were still some women who were, um, on the menu.

A beautiful girl came up to us. Short, jet-black hair, gorgeous tanned skin, perfect smile. "How are you doing?" she asked me in English that indicated she knew the difference between shirts and church.

"Great, thanks, how are you?" I asked, hoping she just happened to be a smoking-hot girl who liked talking to me and had no ulterior motives.

We talked for a few minutes, and the conversation turned to the little village in Thailand that she was from, how much she loved living in the big city, and how she enjoyed going to the beach on the weekend to swim.

It was like a normal conversation I'd have with anyone else, but with the underlying message that in the next half hour I could have her in my hotel room for a mere twenty-five dollars.

I felt it only right to tell her the truth. "I don't want you to waste time with me tonight and not make money. But just so you know, I won't be bringing you back to my hotel room."

She laughed. "That's fine. I just enjoy talking to you. It's a change of pace to have someone who just wants to talk." Wow. I actually felt like a good, moral person for once.

Pat finished his beer first and was heading back to the hotel. Without a prostitute.

John called out to him: "You're really not gonna get a girl?" And Pat said, "No, of course not. You remember meeting my wife, right?"

I still had some beer left to finish, so I said goodnight to Pat.

Now it was just John and me. The girl I'd been talking to left to get a drink. John looked at me. "You gonna bring her back?"

"No," I said, "we're just hanging. I already told her that's not why I'm talking to her."

He looked shocked, like he'd seen a ghost. "Really? You're not gonna get a girl?"

I didn't want to get into an entire defense about why I wasn't hiring a prostitute and how just because something feels good doesn't mean you should do it.

Yet the environment had totally sucked me in. John was getting a prostitute, as were a lot of the guys around us. It's not like there was a stigma attached to it here. No judgment at all.

Nonetheless, I was calling it a night. I said good-bye to the beautiful Thai girl, and then said good-bye to The John.

I walked back to the hotel on my own as women on the street asked if I needed a date. And though the real answer was, "Yes, desperately so," I still said no.

I got back to the room, took a cold shower—not for virtuous purposes, but because the hot water had run out—and lay on my bed.

A voice in my head kept saying, "Come on, go back to the bar! The girl is amazing, she's sweet, she looked clean, and you'd never miss the twenty-five dollars! No one is going to find out. You're in Thailand."

The temptation was so strong, but then another voice spoke up: "What's wrong with you, Lino? You're Catholic. You know it's wrong; you know it's a mortal sin. This shouldn't even be a fight!"

I felt guilty for even being tempted. "Lino," I said to myself, "a good Catholic isn't tempted by this sort of thing. It should be, at most, a passing thought. But you're really torn right now. I don't imagine most devout Catholics have to fight this fight. Seriously, something is wrong with you..."

And with those pleasant thoughts, I went to sleep.

When I woke up the next morning, I had to laugh at myself. I had won a battle, if not the war. But hey, I didn't hurt my relationship with God.

I fought, I struggled, and I won—and I didn't give into temptation. Not exactly on my way to canonization, but I'm always grateful to God when I don't fall.

11

Goob

"I bought a Japanese car the other day. Turned on the radio. I didn't understand a word they were saying!"

It's a Rodney Dangerfield joke. I told it to some friends in the fall of 1987, walking down the halls of my Catholic high school, and one guy laughed harder—and longer—than the rest. And we've been friends ever since.

His real name is Paul, but everyone calls him Goob. Something about when he was a little kid he liked to eat Little Goober candies. I've never really learned the story because it's not about me and I quickly lose interest in those types of stories.

We graduated from high school in 1989 and headed off to the same Catholic university. We were roommates sophomore, junior, and senior year. We were roommates the year after graduation as well, just for good measure.

In 1995, Goob wanted a change of pace and moved to Alaska. That's the kind of dude he is. He found himself in the town of Wasilla. Yes, the Wasilla that Sarah Palin made famous when she announced she would be running with John McCain in 2008. I had visited him there a few times and had hazy memories of drinking and fishing. Not much else to do there. Fish. Drink. Run for vice president.

Goob is one of my best friends. We hang out only once a year, but when we do, it's a doozy.

* * *

In the late '90s, I was "in between jobs" and living at my parents' home. The phone rang.

The voice on the other end said a simple: "Linoooo…"

"Goobooo," I replied. "What is happening, my white friend?" Goob, for the record, is pretty white.

After a few minutes of catching up, it turned out he had a proposal: "I'm flying from Alaska to Minnesota. A guy is paying me to pick up a car and drive it back here for him."

Sounded shady. "We'll drive straight north to Canada and all the way across the country till we get to Alaska."

I needed a map.

"This is definitely a two-man job," Goob said. "Come on, let's do it. It'll be fun. We'll figure out what we're supposed to be doing with our lives. Maybe we'll find love. I've got it: We'll figure out the meaning of life."

I'm always searching for meaning. Sometimes I try hard; sometimes not at all. But I really do want to find out what this life is all about.

Plus, someone was gonna pay meals, hotels, gas, and give us a little spending money.

"OK, Goob, let's do it. A road trip to discover the meaning of life."

"Great, Lino. I'll see you in three weeks. God bless."

Oh, that's right. I forgot to mention that since Goob moved to Alaska, he had become an Evangelical. Or nondenominational. Or something like that. Now that he was much more into God, I thought that would help in our search for meaning.

* * *

The vehicle we'd be driving was a slightly used, red GMC Suburban. "It's just like me," were the first words out of Goob's mouth. "Big, fat, red, and looking for trouble."

"It's a battering ram, Goob. That's not something I want to say about a vehicle."

Most of the trip is a blur, but I kept a diary. I had originally planned to write a book based on our adventures and the insights we gained from the trip. These are my actual entries of that week.

* * *

Monday

8:52 AM. 81,885 miles on the odometer. Leaving Brainerd, Minnesota.

12:30 PM. Thief River Falls, Minnesota. We stop at Artco. The place they make Arctic Cat snowmobiles. We joined fourteen other folks on a tour of the factory to see how Goob's favorite snowmobile is made. This was the most boring tour of my life. I hoped to get skewered by the forklift lady and end my misery.

3:00 PM. Goob and I were just talking about God. Though we were both raised Catholic, we've been turned off by the Church lately. It doesn't seem to relate to our lives. Whatever church he's involved with, I have to admit Goob seems much closer to God now. He reads the Bible every day and seems to have a deeper relationship with God. I'll never stop being Catholic, but I want what he seems to have spiritually. We'll definitely have to talk more about this. We've got a whole week of nothing but car time.

6:00 PM. Arrived in Brandon, Manitoba. Just saw a road sign: "Slam dunk your junk." Not sure what it means. Sounds painful.

9:00 PM. Checked into hotel and went to bar next door. Am drinking a beer named Club as I write this. The beer is slightly chilled but not cold. Have to drink them fast so they don't get warm. Met a guy named Corey who heard we're driving to Alaska. "I'll go with you guys," he announced. He wants to stay in our room for the night and then have us stop by his place tomorrow to pick up some of his clothes. We really shouldn't bring dudes we meet at the bar along with us.

10:00 PM. According to our bartender, Chelsea, there are more barbecues in Canada than the whole United States. Not per capita, but actual barbecues. That can't be right.

* * *

Tuesday

9:40 AM. Set alarm clock for 8:00. Alarm went off at 9:30. How is that possible? Goob is in shower right now, but we're running late.

10:30 AM. Stopped at gas station for breakfast. Bought some King Dons. They looked like Ding Dongs. Same wrapper, same taste. Odd.

12:15 PM. Outside of Regina. Rhymes with a certain word, but Goob and I always say it wrong. We also laugh every time we hear someone say it. We're immature. Listening to 104.9 FM, where the voice guy says over and over again, "The wolf rocks Regina." For some reason, that's funny to me.

4:15 PM. Just drove by the "S & M Family Restaurant." That's a poorly thought-out name for a "family" restaurant. They should rename that.

5:26 PM. Listening to Bruce Springsteen's "Blood Brothers." That's how I feel about Goob. He's my blood brother. It's the type of thing I want to tell him, but I don't know how to express it right now. Instead, I'm writing it here. Girls seem to be able to express their feelings to one another more easily than guys do.

7:30 PM. Arrived in Lloydminster. Getting petrol, but decided to stay the night in town. Just heard that the hotel we're staying at has a strip club in the basement. How ridiculous is that?

* * *

Wednesday

10:20 AM. Hotel last night did, in fact, have a strip club in the basement. We went and met the least enthusiastic stripper in the world. She did sit with us and have a drink, though, and she seemed nice. Her stage name was Brooke, but we found out her real name is Sylvia. I felt bad for her. And bad for us. If this trip is all about finding the meaning of life, we took a step backward last night.

12:57 PM. Stopped at a Harley-Davidson dealership. Guy tried to tell us a joke: "What do a pizza and a girl have in common?" But he didn't remember the punch line.

5:00 PM. Stopping in Edmonton for the night. Going to Planet Hollywood for dinner and then gonna take it easy. Tired. Long drive tomorrow.

* * *

Thursday

10:23 AM. Just woke up. Last night was insane. After dinner, walked by Club Malibu. The bouncer said they were having a bikini contest. "Do you want to be judges in the bikini contest?" he asked. The crowd was crazy. The big-screen TVs played loops of nothing but hockey fights. Guys in the corner with long hair, rockin' out to "Rock and Roll All Nite." The judges were us and an eighteen-year-old named Phil. Or Bill. Couldn't tell. It was so loud, and he was so drunk. Afterward, he said, "Let's exchange our addresses." You know you're drunk when guys are exchanging home addresses. Even the bartender was drinking.

11:30 AM. Breakfast at Tim Horton's. Donuts. We asked for directions, and the guy said, "You can follow me." Canadians are the nicest people.

3:00 PM. Outside of Fox Creek. The hangover is disappearing.

8:00 PM. Had dinner at A & W. Just gonna watch TV tonight. We've really gotta start talking about life and what it's all about.

* * *

Friday

9:30 AM. Goob brought some beers to the room last night. I thought we weren't gonna drink, but I was wrong. Just got in car; breakfast is King Dons, Twinkies, Munchos, orange juice, Mountain Dew. I feel like crap.

10:00 AM. Smoking a cigar, windows rolled down, and nothing in front of us but the open road.

10:05 AM. Mountains are beautiful. Goob says he's reminded of God's power and glory in creation. "Excuse us. We're just passing through." Not me, I don't feel close to God in nature.

10:50 AM. Passing a guy riding his Harley, with a dog in the sidecar like Batman and Robin. We make up how that conversation went.

Owner: "Hey, buddy, wanna go for a ride?"

Dog: "Woof! Great!"

Owner: "Let's drive to Alaska!"

Dog: "Woof! Dammit!"

12:54 PM. Lunch at A&W. Saw an old married couple. That's the only way to tell if you have a successful marriage: when you're old. Not sure how to determine it the first few decades.

4:10 PM. Some Japanese guys are biking. We drive by one of them, honk, and wave. He smiles and waves. Another mile up, another guy. Another smile and wave. Their arms are probably more tired from waving than their legs are from biking.

6:42 PM. Leaving Liard River Hot Springs. Met an eighty-three-year-old guy. Both knees had metal plates and he's had four bypasses. I don't want to get old.

* * *

Saturday

10:00 AM. In the car. Eating donuts, Pop-Tarts, orange juice, and Mountain Dew. Only had four drinks last night. Took it easy.

11:40 AM. Driving by Screw Creek. Why name it that?

3:00 PM. Listening to Frank Sinatra. Those were the days. Smoking was good for you. So was drinking. You woke up in the morning still wearing your tuxedo from the night before.

4:00 PM. Tired. Just lit another cigar, turned the music up, trying to get energized.

4:40 PM. Tape player stopped working. Been an hour since we saw anything. If the car were to break down around here, we're out of luck.

1:30 AM. We're in Whitehorse. Just got back from the bar. The bartender was a girl who was every dude's dream. Except for mine. Cute, yeah. But with a hard edge to her. Harley-Davidson T-shirt. Could fix her own plumbing. Not a euphemism for something, either—there was a leak at the sink behind the bar while we were there and she actually fixed it.

Goob and I made some friends at the bar. As we were leaving, a guy said "Wait, I've got something for you." He returned with a painting he had done. It was of a man vomiting in the toilet. Nice.

* * *

Sunday

11:15 AM. Really hung over.

12:15 PM. Just saw the "Welcome to Alaska" sign. Pulled over and took a picture.

12:30 PM. Crossed the border. Lonely customs guy really wanted to chat. We just want to go home.

1:05 PM. Just bought four tacos for a dollar. These won't taste good.

4:20 PM. Waiting in construction. We're only seventy-nine miles from Wasilla. So close.

6:30 PM. We made it. 85,050 miles on the odometer. Too tired to add up how many miles we drove.

* * *

When we left for the trip, I thought we'd find the meaning of life, and then I'd write a book about it. Instead, based on alcohol intake and food consumption, I probably took a year off my life. And our insights perhaps could have been made into a very small pamphlet. But, boy, did we have fun.

The truth is, I know the meaning of life. The meaning of life is to love. To lay down your life for those you love. As Saint John of the Cross says: "In the evening of our lives, we will be judged by how we loved."

But I'm always out searching for a different meaning of life. One that is somehow more complicated and yet simpler at the same time. It's as if, because I was raised Catholic and it's always been a part of my life, I'm searching for something that's been in front of me the whole time.

I don't know how I'll answer to God for all the time I've wasted and the good I could have done in this world but didn't. I know I need to get busy "loving" more.

Oh, and by the way, I never told Goob that the Japanese-car joke wasn't my own. Friendships built on crazy humor, booze, and bad food seem to be the strongest.

12

Adventures in Confession: Part Two

In the late '90s, a friend told me that Mother Teresa would go to confession as often as once a week. Considering that I *knew* I was a bigger sinner than she was, I decided to start going more frequently.

And if you're anything like me, God forbid, sexual sins are the toughest sins to confess. I would rather say I killed a man with my bare hands than admit to sexual sins committed by those hands.

I figure that sexual sins are what priests hear about most often in confession. I've never asked any of my priest friends, it's just a guess based on…well, me. Not exactly a scientific poll. And I realize I should refrain from using the word *poll* when talking about sexual sins.

Like most people (guys), I might think about a particular set of sins before going to confession, some of them sexual. Before confessing, however, I examine my conscience. And what do you know? I discover lots of other sins: judging others, not honoring my parents, being envious of what others have, gossiping. Yippee for me! More to confess!

Sometimes I get so discouraged that I wonder if I should keep going to confession. But I know I can live the right way only with God's help. Being in a state of mortal sin doesn't advance the cause. I've gotta give God's grace every chance I can to work in me.

* * *

Because confession is such a humbling experience, I'm always a behind-the-screen penitent.

I went face-to-face once, primarily because the priest was a friend of mine and I knew he'd recognize my voice anyway. Also, I didn't have any mortal sins to confess. If anything, I thought he'd be impressed with my piety. He wasn't.

It was incredibly awkward because he's my friend. But now he was acting *in persona Christi,* in the person of Christ, to absolve me of my sins.

"Bless me, Father, for I have sinned," I began. As soon as we made eye contact, I thought I was going to laugh. So I had to stare at the floor the whole time. I might as well have been behind the screen.

After that experience, I realized I would always go behind the screen. Face-to-face is too difficult. I'm talking to God, and being forgiven through His minister, the priest, but the priest isn't there to judge me. I figure there's no need for him to know it's me, so why show my face? And why not change my voice, too, while I'm at it?

Yeah, I've been guilty of changing my voice. That's because I learned my lessons the hard way.

I once worked at a parish that, like most Catholic parishes, had a regular schedule for confession. It had been a couple months since my last confession and I had tallied up some sins, but I didn't want to confess my sins to my coworkers. Even though they were priests.

Being an employee, I had a schedule of which priest was hearing confessions when. There was a retired priest who would help out on occasion, and I knew he was a bit hard of hearing so I jumped at the chance.

Standing in line, I saw his name on the confession door and knew I'd be safe. I went in, said, "Bless me, Father, for I have sinned," and began my confession. I had some particularly embarrassing sins in there, and I was glad I was confessing them to a stranger.

After confessing my sins, I concluded with the traditional "For these sins, and all the sins of my past, I am sorry."

It was now time for some words of counsel from the priest before he gave me my penance.

He began to speak. "Let's thank God for the grace of a good confession…"

Uh-oh. I recognized his voice immediately. He was my boss. Now thankfully, it's not like I confessed stealing office supplies, but if I recognized *his* voice so quickly…and we'd now worked together a number of years…I was afraid he recognized *my* voice.

Later that afternoon, at a staff meeting, let's just say I was rather quiet.

After that, I created a "confession voice." It's low and deep. I revealed it on the air, and the consensus was that I sound like the creepy guy from *The Silence of the Lambs* requesting that lotion be put in a basket.

Before you judge me for changing my voice, however, here's one more story with my pre-"confession voice."

I was struggling with a particular sin a few years back, and, not wanting to go to confession at my workplace, I went to a nearby parish.

Once every week or two, I'd stop by, confess my sins, and head back to work. This pattern continued for months.

It was the same priest in the confessional each time, though I did appreciate that he regularly changed up my penance. Made me feel like he really didn't know it was me and wasn't tired of me showing up.

One particularly depressing confession, after I wrapped up my sins, the priest began his words of counsel with, "Well, as I've said before..."

You've gotta be kidding me. "As I've said before..."? That meant that he recognized my voice... This was horrific, and it was all I needed to ensure I would no longer use my real voice.

Another thing I've learned over my years of confession is that it's best to speak quietly when confessing my sins. If there's a line of people behind me, I always try to talk real quietly, just loud enough for the priest to kinda understand me. He may not know if I said I killed a guy (like a murderer) or billed a guy (like an accountant). If he has follow-up questions, he'll ask 'em. But I don't want anybody walking by the confessional and overhearing what I have to say.

By the way, just a quick note to priests hearing confessions: If confessions start at 5:00 PM, any chance you could get there a few minutes early, before the line forms? Or if that's not possible, how about staring down at the ground as you enter the confessional?

There's nothing worse than standing in line, waiting for the priest to arrive, and having him show up, stare at each of the people in line, and then go in. Kind of ruins the whole anonymity thing.

I'm truly sorry for my sins. I really am. I want to be reconciled with God and have His grace in my life. That's why I'm in the confessional. I just don't want anybody knowing it's me.

13

Roommates

I received the sacrament of Confirmation in eighth grade—and then promptly left the Church.

I've got a group photo of my classmates and me following our confirmation by Bishop Robert Carlson, the auxiliary bishop of St. Paul–Minneapolis at the time. I'm on the edge of the shot looking to run away. He had confirmed me and in doing so gave me the freedom to leave the Church. Yay!

What our confirmation teacher said was: "You are confirmed in the Catholic faith. You are adults. This means the faith is your own and it's up to you to live it out."

What we heard was: "Your parents aren't going to force you to come to church anymore."

So I took some time off. I didn't stage a protest against Catholicism. I wasn't anti-Catholic, nor did I have a problem with a particular doctrine or discipline. I was just a lazy teenager who didn't see how the Church fit into my life.

After being confirmed, I moved on from the public junior high to a Catholic high school. My sophomore year, Bishop Carlson visited to offer Mass for the student body. My buddy Charlie and I wanted to give him a warm welcome. Neither of us was particularly religious, but we did like religious figures.

Charlie and I shared a locker, and we had hanging in it an eight-by-ten of Pope John Paul II that Charlie fake-autographed, saying: "To Lino and Charlie, thanks for all the good times. John Paul II."

In keeping with this irreverence, we came up with something for Bishop Carlson's visit. Our uniforms consisted of polyester-blend trousers and starched, blue button-down shirts, but we were allowed to wear T-shirts underneath. So we had T-shirts made to show him our appreciation: When the appropriate moment came, we'd "flash" the bishop with shirts that said "I ♥ Bishop Carlson."

It goes without saying that neither of us knew the theological significance of a bishop. The fact is that they are successors to the twelve apostles who were chosen by Jesus. The apostles then appointed and ordained successors, who appointed and ordained their own successors, and so on. The bishop today has a direct line of apostolic succession all the way back to Jesus.

But Charlie and I weren't honoring apostolic succession. We thought it'd be worth a quick laugh, maybe get girls laughing with—instead of at—us. So who's the victim?

Mass was held in the auditorium. This was like a home game for me since I was a theater guy. I knew the best seats, the lighting grid, and even how to run the fog machine if necessary. We had a decent chance of getting the bishop's attention.

Toward the end of the Mass, it was time for Charlie and me to shine. As the bishop looked over, we unbuttoned our shirts and showed our love.

He raised his hand—though we weren't sure if it was to strike us or bless us—smiled and...blessed us. Cool.

The principal couldn't suspend us for the gag because apparently the bishop liked it.

* * *

In the mid-2000s I was doing freelance work for the United States Conference of Catholic Bishops. I was going to Washington, D.C., for the bishops' meetings where I'd be conducting a weeklong series of television and radio interviews.

As I boarded the plane in Minnesota on an early morning, I bumped into some friends of mine who do youth ministry.

"Hey, Lino, you going to the meetings?" Tom asked.

"Yeah, doing a bunch of interviews. What about you guys?"

"Going to kiss up to bishops and ask for money."

Gotta love honesty.

"Well, great, let's hang out on someone else's tab," I said.

We landed, shared a cab to the hotel, and made our plan.

Tom said, "I'll stop by your room at seven, we'll have dinner, drinks, and a nice cigar."

"Sounds like a plan to me," I replied. This hanging out with bishops ain't so bad.

When I got to my hotel room, I did my usual routine of cleaning the place with antibacterial wipes, working over every door handle, remote control, and light switch. If a human being touched it, I'm cleaning it. I then showered in case I picked up any germs along the way. The hour-long OCD tasks done, I got down to the actual work they were paying me for.

I went to the main lobby with my D.C.-based television crew to look for our first victim, uh, interview.

"Lino, my brother!"

I knew that voice. Few guys call me their brother. It had to be Doug.

"Lino!" he was yelling. Most of the bishops, their secretaries, other journalists, even deaf folks were looking over at the guy screaming my name. *Lino* is such a strange-sounding word that it could be code for something. Maybe it's a safe word. No one knows.

Doug and I were twenty yards away from each other, but he had his arms open wide running toward me. It's as if we were in a field, the golden sun hitting our skin, the wind blowing through our hair, as we ran toward each other.

Except I wasn't running; I was waiting, bracing myself for the embrace.

Doug's got a heart of gold, and he's one of the nicest people in the world. You can't *not* smile when you're around him. Unless you're around him for more than five minutes.

"How are you, my brother? What are *you* doing here?"

Considering I had a camera guy, producer, and soundman with me, I'd have thought the answer would be obvious.

"Doing some TV work, Doug."

"No kidding?"

"What are you up to?" I actually had valid reason to ask. He was dressed in a suit and had a small microphone in his hand, but no one else was around him.

"I'm doing some Internet work."

That's the worst part about the Internet: Anyone can "work" in the Internet, but are you making money? Is it a dot com? Videos only seen in Germany? It's very vague.

"Well, that's great, Doug."

"You're staying at *this* hotel?" The tone in his voice made it sound like only the richest of the rich could possibly afford to stay here.

"Yeah," I responded, "all the meetings are here. The bishops are staying here. So it just made the most sense. Why?"

"I wish I were staying here. The place was all booked so I'm like twenty miles away. In the ghetto."

There's a word you don't hear enough. Ghetto.

"Real bad part. All sorts of ethnicities there." Though Doug is an ethnic type himself, I took it from his tone that it must be the *wrong* sort of ethnicities.

"Yeah, it's like a fifty-dollar cab ride each way. So I'll take a cab here every morning, stay all day, and then cab it back to the ghetto."

At this point, Catholic guilt got the best of me. Not that guilt is bad. It's a reminder to my conscience that either I'm doing something wrong…or not doing something I could be doing. In this case, it was me realizing that I had a big, comfortable room while poor Doug was traveling back and forth.

Doug's a good guy and a better Catholic. He's a guy who knows Catholicism in terms of theology, but more important, he knows God, not just about God.

He also has great belief in the devil, and whenever things don't go well? He blames Satan. "The devil doesn't want it, Lino," was a common refrain.

"Doug," I'd argue, "why did the devil want my burger to be well done instead of medium well? This is Fuddrucker's, and I don't see the Prince of Darkness as the franchisee here."

"The devil is always finding a way to discourage us," he'd say.

Doug's right, of course, and that faith in good and evil is another thing that I love about him.

"Tell you what," I offered. "How about we go get you an extra room key? You'll have a place to keep your stuff so you don't have to carry it back and forth to the 'ghetto,'" I said using air quotes. "Plus, it's a double room and I'll be out all day, so for all I care you can use the other bed, take a nap in the afternoon, whatever you want."

"Oh, thanks, brother!" Another big hug.

We got Doug a room key, said good-bye, and went on to our own work. Around six, finished with my interviews, I was done for the day. The plan was to relax, watch some TV, and take a shower before the guys came to my room at seven.

About six-forty-five there's a knock at my door. The guys are a little early, and I hadn't had time to shower, but I answered the door anyway... to find Doug.

"Hey, Doug, what's up?"

"I'm taking you up on your offer!" he said, all smiles.

"What offer?" I asked. I looked down and saw his luggage with him.

"To stay with you this week! I checked out of that hotel in the ghetto."

I considered slamming the door shut, but then I remembered he had a key. If anything, the knock was just a courtesy.

"Oh, OK, come on in."

Doug dragged in two huge bags.

"What's with all the luggage, Doug? You on the lam?"

"No, after my week in D.C., I'm off to Rome for another week of meetings and interviews." Great. The guy had two weeks' worth of clothing, all being unloaded in my room.

He plopped the bags on what had now become his bed, and started unpacking. He was eyeing the closet space. "You need all these hangers? I've gotta get all my suits on hangers."

"Well," not sure how to state the obvious, "the clothes I've got on the hangers I kind of need to use."

"Come on, some of your shirts don't need hangers. Your jeans definitely don't. I've got suits here, man!"

"OK, yeah, I guess." I felt bad that I had presumed to use my own hangers. I'm just as selfish as everyone says. "Make yourself at home. I'll try not to get in your way. I'm gonna clean up."

As I took my shower, I tried to remember Bible passages about welcoming my neighbor. About being charitable. About doing it with a cheerful heart. It wasn't coming easily to me. I usually do the right thing grudgingly, but I know God doesn't want a grumpy, mildly charitable heart. He wants me to have a joyful, completely charitable heart.

I recalled Jesus saying that if someone asks for your cloak, give him your tunic too. Maybe there's a correlation. I gave Doug my key, so why not give him my room, too.

Hospitality is the next topic I considered. Jesus said something about taking in the stranger. Well, let's be honest, I'm never gonna let a total transient in my home. Maybe Doug is the closest I can get. The Son of Man didn't have a place to lay His head, and if Doug didn't stay with me, he wouldn't either.

I'd run through every theological concept I could think of in the course of a five-minute shower, and I came to peace with the decision.

As I got out of the shower, I heard a knock at the door.

"I'll get it," Doug said.

He opened the door, and there was Tom, the guy who was on the flight with me, who saw me check in by myself. Now he was looking at a young man in T-shirt and shorts.

"Uh," I heard Tom through the bathroom door, "I think I have the wrong room. Is Lino here?"

Doug replied, "Yeah, of course. Lino! Your friend is here!"

Sheepishly, I answered, "OK, you can let him in. I'll be right out."

I could only imagine what was going through Tom's mind. "What's up with Lino? Leave the guy alone for five hours and he has a manservant in his room?"

A few minutes later, I came out. Of the bathroom, that is. I quickly got dressed, and was on my way.

"Umm, I'll be back later. Not too late." I couldn't believe I was trying to apologize for my schedule in my own hotel room.

"OK," Doug replied, "I'm wiped out, so I'll be calling it a night pretty early."

"I'll try not to wake you when I get back to my, uh, our room," I said.

Tom and I walked down the hall in complete silence. "So you're probably wondering who the guy was, right?" I finally offered.

"Yeah, that was kind of a surprise."

I told him the story. He seemed to believe me. And we headed out to dinner. A steak, several drinks, and a cigar later, I returned to the room.

I'm not sure what I dreaded more: Coming in and having Doug say, "Where have you been? I've been worried sick about you!" Or finding him asleep, which meant I'd have to stumble through the room in darkness, guided only by the light coming from my cell phone.

It was the latter. Fine.

The next morning I woke at 6:30 to the television blaring. I looked up and saw Doug, wearing only a pair of boxers, ironing his clothes for the day. Apparently the hangers didn't do their job.

"Doug, what the hell? I'm sleeping."

"Oh, I'll be out of here in a while. Right after I do morning prayer. Want to pray with me?"

"Uh, no," I said. And went back to sleep.

* * *

It went like this all week. Late nights for me; early mornings for Doug—and thus me.

But I felt like a better Christian, because I did the right thing. The Holy Spirit was kinda guiding me—and for once, I let Him.

As Doug and I were checking out of the room, there was someone else checking out a few doors down.

It was Bishop Carlson. He was no longer the auxiliary bishop of St. Paul–Minneapolis; he was now archbishop of St. Louis.

"Excuse me, Archbishop?" I asked, walking toward him.

"Yes?" he answered with a big smile.

"Hey, my name is Lino Rulli. You wouldn't remember it, but you confirmed me back at St. Ambrose parish in St. Paul, Minnesota."

"Great," he responded.

"Well, I just wanted to reintroduce myself. Thanks for confirming me."

"You're welcome."

I decided not to bring up the "I ♥ Bishop Carlson" T-shirts. Or my roommate Doug.

14

Wet Behind the Ears

All Italian families should have a lawyer and a bishop in the family. It makes life a lot easier and more entertaining.

My cousin became an archbishop in 2000. It was weird having a family member who was owed a certain amount of respect I wasn't willing to give other cousins.

Just a week after becoming an archbishop, he was going to preside at the baptism of my cousin Lori's daughter, Sofia.

I had asked other family members whether we were required to kiss his episcopal ring. A bishop wears a ring as a sign of the authority given to him as a successor to the apostles. People can kiss it as a sign of respect for the office he holds, but I didn't know if it was still the custom. Even if it was, I didn't want to do it. Mostly because I'm a germophobe.

First I asked my aunt. "What's the protocol here? Does everyone kiss the ring?"

"Well," she said hesitantly, "he is an archbishop, and it's quite an honor to have an archbishop in the family."

That was a yes. I went to some of my other cousins.

"Well," they'd say, "he is an archbishop, and it's quite an honor…"

"OK," I'd interrupt, "the 'well' is all I needed to hear." The answer was yes. When I saw him, I positioned my giant nose to avoid impact and I kissed the ring.

The baptism was a typical Italian scene. The opening hymn went on too long. The homily went on too long. As for the baptism itself—just think: This little baby had original sin washed away. She was now part of the Christian faith. It was a completely supernatural experience in the natural course of the day.

After the ceremony, we had an enormous five-hour meal celebrating Sofia's entry into the Body of Christ.

During one of the breaks between courses, I told my archbishop cousin that I was going to be going to Israel. I thought he'd be happy to hear that a family member was going on such a pilgrimage.

"We'll be visiting Jerusalem, Bethlehem, the Sea of Galilee," I said. "Oh, and I'll be getting rebaptized in the Jordan River."

"Lino," he replied in his broken English, "Thees, thees ees no posseeble."

I was confused. "Why isn't it possible? I already submitted my down payment and everything."

"Uh, to bee bap-ah-tized-uh again, a second-ah time, thees, thees, cannot-uh happen."

Now I was more confused. I understand Italian-ish speak, and if I weren't lazy I would have had the conversation in actual Italian.

"Yeah," I argued, "but I was a baby when I was baptized; I don't remember any of it, so this will be my chance to do it for real."

"No, no, no," he said, hitting the palm of his hand on his knee, the way you would slap your knee after a funny joke. But he wasn't laughing. "Thees cannot-uh happen."

Turns out that when you're baptized in the name of the Father, Son, and Holy Spirit, it's a one-time deal. This is probably something I should have learned at some point earlier in my life. Maybe I slept through theology class that day. And since baptism is once and for all, I soon realized I wouldn't be rebaptized, but I would be renewing my baptismal vows.

* * *

A few months later, in mid-January, fifty of us left on a pilgrimage to the Holy Land (or as a Jewish friend of mine once pointed out: "It's OK to call it *Israel*, Lino"). The flight from Minneapolis–Chicago–New York–Tel Aviv took just under thirty-five hours, but we finally got there.

Our tour bus driver picked us up from the airport in Tel Aviv and drove us to Jerusalem. Along the way, I looked out my window and saw a few donkeys walking on a dirt path.

I turned to the guy next to me and said, "Wow. Just think. That donkey had parents. And those donkeys had parents. If we could go back far enough, it's possible that one of these donkeys' ancestors was the very animal that Jesus rode into Jerusalem on Palm Sunday."

The jet-lagged pilgrim next to me had no interest in the "donkey begat donkey" conversation, though he undoubtedly realized he was sitting next to an ass. Nonetheless, I was in the land that Jesus walked and I knew that spending time in the places where He had lived—a real human being with a specific time and place in history—would increase my faith. I just had to be careful not to push the donkey stuff too much.

At the hotel, the tour guide directed us to our rooms. None of my friends wanted to go on pilgrimage with me, and I couldn't afford to pay the extra money for a single-room supplement, so I was assigned a roommate.

Tom was a middle-aged Midwesterner, a very nice guy who smelled a bit like old cheese. Not too pungent, but just enough that you noticed when he was around.

"Hi, Tom," I said. "Nice to meet you; I'm Lino."

"Hi, Roomie!" he said, with a chuckle and a sweaty handshake.

We got to our room and saw two small single beds roughly five inches apart from each other. No television. A small bathroom. This would be our accommodations for the next several days.

It's one thing for kids to share a room or bunk beds when they go to camp. It's quite another thing for adults to share a room when they go on pilgrimage.

Our first night was similar to what I imagine newlyweds in the Middle Ages experienced on their first night together. No one was there to guide you; you just closed your eyes and hoped for the best.

Every pilgrimage company I'm familiar with offers a list of dos and don'ts for the pilgrims, covering things like passports, availability of ATMs—but nothing on bedtime etiquette. Let alone what to wear.

Pajamas are things dudes shouldn't own. I've never understood pajamas that look more like a sports coat and slacks, with a breast pocket that could hold a handkerchief. It's unclear if the gentleman is meeting with shareholders or the sandman. And sleeping in the nude is not an acceptable option. T-shirt and shorts seems the most appropriate bedtime attire, though I always look more like I'm ready for the gym than for sleep.

Tom went with the most practical, if oddest, outfit—exactly what he was wearing on the flight: button-down shirt tucked into his pants, belt, socks, and shoes.

"Good night, Roomie!" he said. Oh, how I wish he'd quit calling me Roomie.

The next morning, the alarm went off at 6:00 AM. As I rolled over to turn it off, there he was, still wearing the exact same outfit as the day before. He threw back the covers and was out the door in thirty seconds.

* * *

We got on the bus and headed to the Jordan River. It was weird to imagine I'd be in the same spot where Jesus stood when John the Baptist baptized Him.

Turns out I wouldn't be in the *exact* same spot because scholars debate where that might be. Some say it's here, others say it's over there, but since this is where the huge souvenir store is, and it's even handicap accessible, this is the place most tourist groups visit.

I took my shoes and socks off, rolled up my pants, and started wading into the water. "I'm in the River Jordan!"

Jesus entered these waters, the heavens parted, and a voice from the heavens said: "This is my beloved Son with whom I am well pleased."

And there I stood, looking up at the sky, hoping I'd hear a voice.

But I didn't.

"Lord," I said in a silent prayer, "I flew thousands of miles. Risked suicide bombers and other stereotypes related to visiting the Middle East. I slept with Tom. I'm now standing in the Jordan River. Come on, God, where are you!? Think what a great Catholic I'd be if I could tell just one story where I absolutely knew it was all real. That you exist. That it's not all a wacky fairy tale."

Still nothing. All I could picture was that moment in Monty Python when the clouds parted left and right and the cartoon image of God the Father showed up. Another feeble attempt at faith on my terms.

My feet were freezing at this point, and as I left the chilly waters, I passed a group of Evangelicals from Brazil coming in to be baptized.

Brazil is the most heavily Catholic country in the world, so I'm guessing some of these folks were baptized Catholic, left the Church, and were now being "rebaptized," as I used to say.

They were wearing their long white robes, but many of the women, being Brazilian, were wearing thongs underneath. Which was so wrong and so right at the same time. As for the guys who went commando under the robes, let's just say apparently they didn't mind shrinkage when it came to their not-rebaptism.

But if, in fact, this was a group of adults just coming into the Christian faith, it's even wilder. Whether it happens in the Jordan River or on Holy Saturday at the Easter Vigil, it's always crazy watching adults get baptized. And here's what goes through my head the whole time: This Christianity thing is real, or it's not. If it's real, this person is becoming a member of the Body of Christ right in front of me. Her sins are being washed away. She's becoming a new creation. If it's not real, it's just a lame wet T-shirt contest. It really can be only one of those two options.

Regardless, I was happy for those folks in the Jordan. I dipped my hand in the water, made the sign of the cross, and renewed my own baptismal promises.

But I do kinda feel ripped off that I don't remember my baptism.

15

Turn and Cough

I'm a worrier. I come from a long line of worriers. My mom is a worrier. I'm half-worrier on my dad's side.

In the Scriptures, Jesus said, "Be not afraid," many times. But me? I'm always afraid. I'm constantly in fear.

As I've mentioned, I'm a germophobe, so I can't shake hands with someone without immediately busting out the hand sanitizer.

When driving, I don't even like taking a left turn if there's traffic behind me. I'm afraid I'm inconveniencing others, which may upset them, and someone might get mad and want to hit me.

And my number one fear: Getting sick.

You know that feeling when you're just getting a cold? Yeah, that's more fearful to me than the cold itself. As soon as my throat starts hurting, I freak out and take 10,000 percent of my daily dose of vitamin C. I'm so orange I look like I've got jaundice. Of course, it never helps. My fears become realized: I get a cold.

Chicken soup or over-the-counter medicines help some people feel better. For me, it's hearing about other people who are ill. My mom can call and say, "You know, your aunt is sick, too," and that brightens my day. I feel consoled knowing I'm not alone in this.

And though there are no records of this in the Bible, I like picturing Jesus and the apostles getting colds. In fact, I'd like to see this in works of art.

Jesus was the Second Person of the Holy Trinity, fully divine, but fully human as well. When I was in grad school studying theology, I focused a lot on Jesus' humanity. My professors noticed this interest of mine and commented on it, but for some reason, I thought it was important. It was fascinating to imagine the Lord with a head cold, all grumpy.

I once proposed writing a paper on "Bodily Functions in Biblical Times" primarily because I thought it would be interesting to reflect on Jesus' humanity. He was like us in all things but sin, the Bible says (cf. Hebrews 4:15). I figured that'd be a fascinating idea to explore. My professors informed me that I was wrong.

Anyway, during my second year of graduate school, I started developing some painful bodily symptoms of my own. Sometimes I had a burning sensation when urinating. Sometimes I had pain in my stomach. My friend Pat offered a nonmedical prognosis: "You're probably gonna die from it." Me being a worrier, it was time to see a doctor.

This was a risky proposition, however, because for the first two decades of my life I had a tendency to kill doctors.

The doctor who was present at the time of my birth? Dead.

The doctor who performed throat surgery on me as a two-year-old (I was two, not him)? Dead.

My pediatrician? Dead.

By time I was in my teens, I experienced role reversal every time I went to a physician. "I have some bad news," I'd say to the doctor. "It appears you don't have long to live."

Nonetheless, I needed to see a doctor, so I called to make an appointment with the local physician in the small town where I was living.

"Hello, Medical Clinic," a voice said.

"Hi, I'd like to make an appointment."

"OK, when would you like to come in?"

"When is the doctor available?"

"I'm free pretty much anytime."

Wait. The doctor was also the receptionist? And his schedule was completely open?

"Umm…" I stalled, weighing my lack of options. "How about tomorrow?"

His response, a little too eager: "Great!"

The next day, he greeted me in the waiting room. Usually a waiting room is so named because patients wait there for doctors. In this case, the doctor was waiting for me.

The doctor/receptionist/janitor was in his mid-thirties, six feet tall, skinny as a rail, with glasses and thinning hair. He looked like the police sketch of every bank robber I've ever seen.

We went from the waiting room to his office. I sat on the examining table, and he began all the normal doctor activities:

He took the stethoscope out of a frozen meat locker and placed it on my exposed skin. "Deep breath in, then out; in, then out," he said.

Then, "Turn and cough." I did. "Again." Wouldn't you love to know how the medical community decided this was the normal way to check a dude's junk?

"And now I'll test your reflexes using this completely Iron Age test—hitting your knee with a hammer." He hit my knee, my leg kicked out and, in a very Three Stooges moment, my foot landed directly on his sternum.

"Ugh," he said, trying to catch his breath. He didn't try the other knee.

"Well, everything seems to be fine," he said. "Thanks for coming in."

"But doctor," I said calmly, "I'm not here for a physical. I set up the appointment because I'm in pain."

"So, what are your symptoms?" he asked, with the same questioning attitude my mechanic has when asking why I brought the car to the shop. Note to all people who know more about cars, bodies, and cable television boxes than I do: I wouldn't be talking to you if I didn't have a problem. Believe me, there's a problem. Just be patient as I explain it, all right?

He listened, put on his plastic gloves, and I knew I'd soon be singing "Moon River." I pleaded my case as to why this wouldn't be necessary, but he insisted. Not even a drink and some witty banter to warm me up and make me more comfortable?

A little probing, jabbing, and exploring, and the procedure was done. I put my pants back on and retrieved whatever dignity either of us had left while I waited for the diagnosis.

"You seem fine to me," Dr. Feelgood said.

"Well, it didn't *feel* fine to me," I thought to myself.

Upon arriving home, I told my roommates about the appointment. "Was this guy even a doctor?" Pat asked. "That's a procedure for fifty-year-olds! Not twenty-two-year-olds!"

To this day, none of my friends visit the doctor's office without being afraid they're going to get The Lino, as the procedure has come to be known.

But the pain was still there, so I called Dr. Strangelove and asked for another appointment. Maybe he'd come up with a different diagnosis.

I arrived at the waiting room and was relieved to see another patient/victim there. This made me feel much better. Dr. Evil and I went back to his office and reviewed my symptoms again. This time he determined it was an STD.

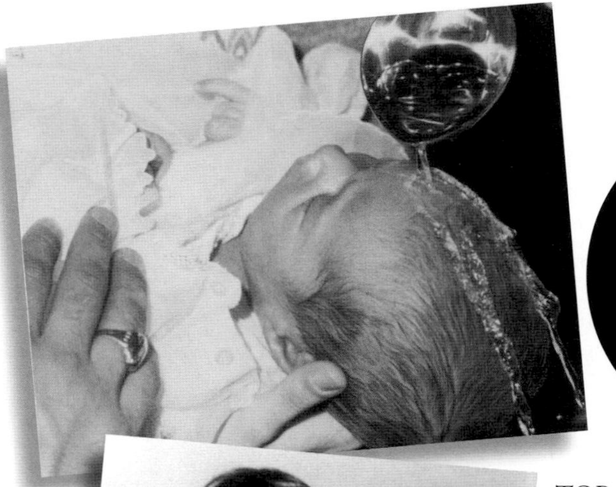

THROUGH THE YEARS WITH Lino Rulli

TOP: *My baptism. I don't remember this day, but really wish I did.*

LEFT: *Perhaps I was a radio prodigy. I'm wearing headphones and my hand is gesturing to make a point.*

BELOW: *I've always been a mamma's boy. (And it's weird seeing my mom as a young woman.)*

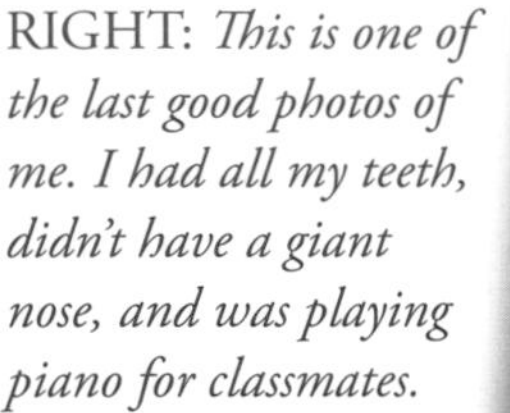

RIGHT: *This is one of the last good photos of me. I had all my teeth, didn't have a giant nose, and was playing piano for classmates.*

BELOW: *My dad, the organ-grinder. And me, the monkey boy. The organ is in the middle.*

LEFT: *My Confirmation day. One of the single worst photos ever taken of a human being.*

ABOVE: *My parents and I after my first starring role in the theater. I was a four-year theater letter winner. Tough to believe I was single in high school.*

LEFT: *Keenan and I in our "punk" years. Please note my "Late Night with David Letterman" shirt: I was a fan even as a punk.*

RIGHT: *My weak attempt at becoming a wrestler. Be grateful you don't have to see me in the singlet.*

BELOW: *My twenty-first birthday. I would no longer be arrested for underage drinking.*

BOTTOM: *Gary Dell'Abate and me in the Bahamas. The picture that would one day lead me to working in satellite radio. Baba Booey! Baba Booey!*

TOP: *Goob and me on the Alaska road trip. Booze may have been consumed before taking this photo.*

ABOVE: *My first Emmy Award. I'm way too excited to have this Golden Idol in my life.*

LEFT: *I grew a beard to travel through Israel and the Palestinian territories. Airport security was kind of tough.*

TOP: *My trip to Petra, Jordan. My cave girl liked me in spite of—or because of—this look.*

ABOVE: *Pops and I in front of Castel Sant'Angelo in Rome. His name is Angelo; my name is Angelo; the castle is named after an angel. That's three angels.*

ABOVE: *Mom and I broadcasting from Vatican Radio. She's always a crowd favorite on the air.*

LEFT: *My grandma and grandpa on their honeymoon at Our Lady of Pompeii; Pompeii, Italy.*

TOP: *Meeting John Paul II, trying to find the right words to say to him.*

ABOVE: *My favorite place on earth: St. Peter's Basilica.*

As a guy working on my master's degree in theology, I saw this as a great accomplishment. In Church circles, everyone knows an STD is a Sacred Theological Doctorate. It was as if I leapfrogged over my master's degree and went right to the doctorate. Fantastic.

Unfortunately, the doctor told me it was an STD, as in "sexually transmitted disease."

The doctor asked me to remove my clothes and put on the hospital gown as he stepped out of the office. Five minutes later, I'm wearing the gown, sitting on the table, and staring blankly around at the misery that is a doctor's office. There's nothing to read, nothing to distract me from my own mortality and sense of helplessness. Being a hypochondriac, I always assume I'm going to die from whatever is ailing me. I started begging God for more time.

"Just let me be OK, Lord, and I'll pray more. I'll love and honor my parents more. I'll be more patient and kind and loving." In a way, I wish I had this driving fear all the time. I'd never waste a minute on sin if I truly kept my mortality and coming judgment before me the way I did in that doctor's office. I honestly think God puts me in these positions to help me correct things in my life that are out of whack.

Meanwhile, Dr. Mengele returned with a sharp, needlelike device. I had no idea what his mysterious plans were. My mind was running wild. What was he going to do with that thing?

Here's how WebMD describes the procedure:

"To collect a sample from the urethra...your doctor will insert a swab into the opening of your urethra."

I'm squirming just reading that.

"Collecting a sample of fluid...may cause mild discomfort or pain."

Placing a metal spike in your urethra causes "mild discomfort or pain"? That's like saying hell is a place of mild discomfort or pain.

"In rare cases, a person may suddenly get dizzy or feel faint (called vasovagal syncope) because of fear or pain when the swab is inserted into the urethra."

Vasovagal syncope? Otherwise known as fainting like a little girl, but completely understandable.

It took perhaps one second to retrieve the sample. One-tenth of a second is how long it took me to start swinging wildly at the doctor like Mike Tyson in his glory days. Body blow, body blow. Shot to the head. Bite his ear off. Anything to get this guy to end the pain.

Minutes later, he licking his wounds and me still wearing a hospital gown, he determined the STD tests were negative, as I had expected. I thought of all those promises I made to God in my panic. Hmm…have to figure out a way to renegotiate those.

* * *

Months later, unsurprisingly, the pain was still there. This time I chose a Catholic doctor in the big city.

Why a Catholic doctor? Because I'm Catholic.

"That's racist, Lino," a non-Catholic friend (as my non-Catholic friends enjoy being called) said.

"Racist?" I said. "It's not racist. If I said I wanted to go to a white doctor because I'm white, that's racist. If I wanted to go to a male doctor because I'm male, that's sexist."

My mind was made up: I go to a Catholic priest to heal my soul. I'm going to a Catholic doctor to heal my body.

After some small talk about my graduate studies, Catholicism, and the beauties of the world, I explained my problem. A pair of gloves, some lube, and a few tears later, I was diagnosed with prostatitis. The symptoms can be similar to those for an STD, so crazy non-Catholic doctor wasn't far off.

After some antibiotics, I was a new man.

I'm happy to report that I occasionally see this doctor at Mass. He's still alive, practicing the faith, and knows more about me than any human being should.

16

Mrs. Lino Rulli

The first time I thought about marriage and settling down was in 1997. I was living in Rome at the time, and my parents had come for a visit.

On the last day of their trip, my dad wanted to visit the Trevi fountain and throw a coin over his shoulder so that he would return to Rome. This is obviously a ridiculous bit of superstition, so Mom stayed behind. As we got to the fountain, I reminded him just how silly this superstition is.

"Pops, I know it's a tradition for tourists to throw a coin in the fountain and they'll get to return to Rome, but think about it: how does throwing a coin over your left shoulder—because God forbid it's the right shoulder—in any way guarantee you'll return to this city?"

"Well, Son," he said, "every time I've visited Rome I've thrown a coin in this fountain, and I've returned every time. Can't argue with success." My dad's funny like that. Another reason I love him.

He's right. I can't argue with success. I *can* argue with superstition, however. Not just because we're Catholic and should place our trust in God rather than superstitions, but because every time my parents spend money uselessly I can't help but think that's less inheritance for me. A coin in a fountain here, a thousand bucks to a palm reader there, and next thing you know my inheritance is nowhere to be found.

For the record, I haven't thrown a coin in the Trevi since the '90s, and I've been back over twenty times.

We bought gelato and took a seat near the fountain for some quality time together.

"So, what's next, Lino?" he asked. I was nearing the end of my stay in the city and had not announced my future plan of action, primarily because I had no plan.

"I don't know, Pops; I feel like life has been really good to me. Graduated college at twenty-one, got my master's degree at twenty-three, I've lived in the Bahamas, and now I'm living in Italy. I'm not sure how to top this."

His answer came immediately, like he'd been waiting to say it. "You know, having a kid is pretty great."

"Well," I said in reply, "I know the process of conceiving a kid is pretty great. Mom might disagree if literally having a child—you know, childbirth—is great."

He paused, perhaps realizing I had a point, but then just repeated himself. "Having a kid is pretty great."

So when Pops said having a kid was great, what I guessed he was really saying was, "Fall in love, get married, have a family, and quit showing off the life you have. Be miserable, like the rest of us."

As soon as he said it, though, I had one girl in mind. Maria.

* * *

I moved to Rome in January 1997. I was twenty-five, a swarthy Italian American, but I couldn't say much more than *ciao* or *spaghetti*, so I decided it was time to learn my mother tongue.

Upon moving there, I immediately enrolled in a beginner's language class. I showed up to the classroom a few minutes early. No one was there, so I stood at the window overlooking a piazza.

I heard a female voice behind me. "Ciao?" It was a questioning "Hello?"—the same intonation you use when answering the phone when your caller ID says "blocked call."

I turned and saw a stunning girl—5'5", long brown hair, beautiful eyes, a great smile. Her dimples had dimples. She was cute, innocent, pure. I wondered to myself how I could defile that pureness. Because I'm a sinner.

I utilized one of my two Italian words in return: "Ciao."

"Ummm…" she paused. "Do you speak English?" I immediately realized she thought I was Italian, maybe even the teacher. I played up the teacher–student fantasy that came to mind.

"Yes, I speak English. And you are?"

"Hi! I'm Maria. I'm sooo excited to be here! I'm from Wisconsin, and I've never been out of the country. Rome is so amazing! The food is great, the people are so nice, I can't believe I'm having this experience." She was talking a mile a minute. "So how long have you been a professor here? You seem pretty young. Well, I'm not trying to hit on you. I just mean, I don't know, I'm so excited. I can't wait to learn…"

Just then, the *real* teacher walked in.

Maria looked at me. Then the teacher. Then back at me.

"Wait," she said, "you're not the teacher?"

I smiled. "Nope, I'm just a guy from Minnesota who's here for the same reasons you are. You kept talking and I couldn't figure out how to interrupt you."

We took our seats and the class began. Two hours later, and with the new ability to say "my eyebrows are brown" in Italian—because God knows that'll be helpful—our first lesson was done.

I said good-bye to Maria and went back to my apartment. I was sharing a great place in the trendy Trastevere neighborhood of Rome with two women, one from France, the other from Germany. It was kinda like the Italian version of *Three's Company*. I was living Jack Tripper's life, complete with regular misunderstandings—commonplace when you don't speak each other's language—and pratfalls.

A few days into school, I was at a café with a classmate, a guy who had known Maria in Wisconsin.

"I think I like that Maria girl," I said, hoping to get the scoop on her. "Is she dating anyone? Does she like swarthy Italian guys? Any felonies?" You know, the regular stuff.

Mike piped up. "Oh, don't waste your time."

"Why's that?" I asked.

"You're not going to get anywhere with her. You'd be lucky to even get a kiss from her after two weeks."

"Really?" I asked, intrigued.

"Yeah," Mike said. "She's a virgin."

It made me more than a little uncomfortable that he knew her sexual history. Or lack thereof. But after hearing that, I liked her even more. Paradoxically, I felt like her virginity was a turn-on. And no, not for the reasons you might think.

It occurred to me that this is what a relationship is about—I like a girl for herself, and she likes me for myself.

The next day I sat next to Maria so we could talk. It was a typical language class—at some point the teacher has us speak in Italian to the person next to us. This was an amazing way to get to know her likes and dislikes without being creepy.

"Tu sei Cattolica?" Are you Catholic?

"Si," she responded. OK, that's good.

"Ti piace vino bianco o vino rosso?" Do you like white wine or red wine?

"Mi piace vino bianco." I like white wine.

"Tu sei una vergine?" Are you a virgin?

OK, I didn't ask that, but I learned an awful lot about her under the guise of practicing the language.

Some of the folks were going out for drinks after class. As soon as I heard Maria was in the group, I volunteered the fact that I'd be joining them. Some wine, some cheese, and some hours later, Maria and I found ourselves alone in a piazza.

"I think you're really awesome," she said.

"I think so, too," I responded.

"It's only been a week, but I already feel like we know each other so well."

I made a mental note to thank the *scuola* for giving me the opportunity to get to know her without being stalker-ish.

"Can I give you a kiss?" I asked.

"Yeah," she said, "but you should know something. I'm a virgin, and I want to wait for sex till marriage."

"That's fine," I responded. "I'm pretty sure we'd be arrested if we did anything more than kiss out here anyway."

Now frankly, I've known lots of women who chose chastity when the person they'd be having premarital sex with was me. I dated a girl once who'd been sexually active with all her previous boyfriends, but after a few dates with me declared: "I want to try chastity for this relationship."

Maria was, for me, the best example of the Church teaching on sexuality that I'd ever met. She wanted to save sex until marriage, but she wasn't weird about it. She wasn't going to become a chastity speaker. She didn't use catch phrases like, "You're worth the wait." She was the sexual equivalent of a nonmilitant vegetarian.

We'd go to church together almost every day, as well—usually St.

Peter's Basilica which was near my apartment. This was in the days before cell phones and texting, so we had to make plans the old-fashioned way: by landline telephone or in person.

"Meet you in the square tomorrow morning at nine?" I'd ask her.

"Sure," she'd say, knowing she'd be about a half hour late, but at least I'd have St. Peter's as my view.

Most days she'd say we should pray together for a few minutes, but that, too, was done in a non-holier-than-thou fashion. She wouldn't say "Lino, let us go and adore our Lord in the Blessed Sacrament for exactly one hour. After our Holy Hour is complete, let us go and serve Him in others." Instead, she'd say, "Want to go to Adoration for a few minutes?" Sure. We'd pray and move on with our day.

We lived on opposite sides of the city, and some nights I'd crash at her place. Because we knew we weren't having sex, sleeping in the same bed was no big deal. It really was just sleeping.

We would lie in bed and say our prayers out loud. To this day, I think about how weird that sounds: a Catholic couple in the same bed, not messing around but saying prayers.

My publisher will warn me not to tell this story because I may be leading people into sin by influencing them to do this. My friends will think I'm an absolute freak that I was in bed with a girl and just prayed. But that was the situation.

* * *

Months into our relationship, and a few days after Pops mentioned how great it was to have kids, Maria and I were out with some friends at a bar and I told my buddy, Bill: "I want to put a ring on that girl's finger." I said it out loud: I wanted to marry her.

I was a student living in Rome, with maybe $1,000 in the bank. No savings, no 401K, and other than two bags of clothes, no possessions.

Not a lot of liquid assets, and maybe it was the liquid courage giving me the strength to even say this.

"How can you afford a ring?" he asked.

"Well, they say the ring should cost ten percent of your salary, right? That means I buy her a hundred dollar ring and tell her my love cannot be measured by karat."

Even I knew that was a bad idea, but note to the guys out there thinking about proposing: If you're buying a ring, don't do it when you get a raise or a new job. Do it when you've got no job. Ten percent of nothing is nothing.

There was only one thing holding Maria and me back from our lifelong commitment of marriage.

The very first time I said "I love you" to her, she was silent. I wondered if I had used too much chloroform. I checked her pulse. Her eyes weren't dilated. She appeared to be just fine, but no response.

"I can't say that back to you," she said. "I'm afraid."

My insecurities were jumping out of me like a man jumping out of a burning building. I was beating myself up: "Why did you tell her you love her? Now she has the upper hand, Lino!"

"I want to say it to you," she said, "but I know what that means. It means you can hurt me more than anyone else. It means there is responsibility. I just can't say it right now. I feel it, but I can't say it."

In a certain way, I had to respect that. She took commitment as seriously as I did. She wouldn't speak of love haphazardly.

But unfortunately, a commitment-phobe like myself was committed to someone who was afraid of commitment.

* * *

Eventually we both left Rome, me to Minnesota and Maria to Wisconsin. We were a couple in theory, but not in reality. We were both too busy living our lives, not finding time for each other, and we drifted apart. We never officially broke up, but it wasn't to be.

A few years later, she called to say she had a new boyfriend.

"What does he do for a living?" I asked, hoping he was a struggling actor or slimy politician.

"He's a sailor." Not like the kind in the navy, serving our country, more like a hybrid of a non-Somalian pirate and Cap'n Crunch. I pictured this sailor of hers wearing a little captain's hat and being an extraordinarily white guy. "Oh, look at me. I'm very white. Look, everyone, how white I am!" I imagined his boat was sponsored by Wonder Bread.

"A sailor in Wisconsin?" I asked, to which she quickly responded, "What, just because you're from Minnesota, land of 10,000 lakes, you don't think we have water?" Clearly a sensitive subject for her.

"I think I'm in love," she said, making sure my heart was broken.

"Have you said 'I love you' to him yet?"

"No," she replied, "but I probably will soon."

We kept in touch, playing a cat-and-mouse game.

A few years later, I got an e-mail. It began with some small talk before hitting the main point.

"News: I'm engaged. He's a great guy and I'm so excited."

I'm rarely happy for other people's happiness. And I couldn't find it in my heart to be happy for her then.

But the thought occurred to me: I should marry her. That would make me happy—and her happy. I should drive to Wisconsin, find her at work, and say, "You can't marry him. Marry me instead." It's a familiar scene in romantic comedies. Always, always works.

I called my buddy Dan to get his advice.

"Hey, you remember that Maria girl I dated a few years ago?" I asked.

"Yeah," he responded, "the girl you didn't have sex with, right?"

"Yeah, yeah, well, it was more than that, but whatever. She's engaged, but I'm thinking of going down and breaking it up. I'll show up at her place, tell her to 'drop the zero and get with the hero' or something like that. And I'll propose to her."

Dan asked a few logical questions. "Do you know where she lives? Do you even have a ring? Are you really gonna use the 'zero–hero' line?"

"Well," I said, "I can figure those things out. When I talk to you on Monday, I'll either be engaged, or she'll still be engaged to the other guy."

I thought about it for a while, but I decided not to go for it. Life isn't a movie, and more than anything, I was afraid of being rejected. My career was going well, and I didn't have time for love.

Most regrettably, I didn't put it to prayer. Who knows what would have happened if I had. Ironically, the person who most encouraged me to pray—Maria—wasn't there to encourage me to pray on this one.

I chose my career over her. In some sense, this book is the fruit of my career: You're holding what could have been my wife.

17

Never Been to a Turkish Prison

"It is not good for man to be alone." That's what God says about Adam in the book of Genesis (Genesis 2:18). And then God creates Eve.

I echo those biblical sentiments every time I go out to eat dinner by myself: It's not good for man to be alone. Especially this man.

July 2005, and I was in Istanbul, Turkey, for the night. I found a nice little restaurant for dinner.

Eating by myself is an odd experience. It's no problem when I'm in the comfort of my own living room eating pizza. But when I eat by myself in public, it's a different story. I try to pick restaurants that appear to have a nonjudgmental clientele. There have to be just enough couples, families, and single people eating there so that I don't stand out too much.

I imagine that folks have a mix of emotions when they see me striding in by myself. Sadness. Confusion. They try not to look. It's kind of my reaction when I see someone in a wheelchair. I don't want to make eye contact and have them become self-conscious, but I don't want to *not* make eye contact and have them think society ignores them.

Sometimes when I go to a restaurant by myself, I'll try to look occupied. I'll bring a notebook along and give the impression I'm a travel-guide writer, or maybe a novelist writing the next great Turkish novel. I may even be a guy so comfortable in his own skin that I don't care what others think of me.

So I was at this restaurant and the hostess seated me at a table for two. It was very sad when the busboy came by and cleared the other place setting. What's the reasoning behind this? Do they really have to make a formal announcement that I'm there by myself? There's no harm in an extra plate and glass across from me, is there? It's basically declaring to the restaurant: "This gentleman has come in by himself. He is neither waiting for someone else, nor does he know anyone else. He is Han Solo for the evening."

The waiter eventually came to my table and started speaking gibberish to me. Well, it wasn't actually gibberish; it was probably Turkish, but I didn't understand a word he said.

After I said, "What?" several times in English, he picked up on the fact that I was American.

"Oh, you're not Turkish?"

"Nope."

"You look Turkish."

"Nope."

"But you are Muslim, yes?"

I thought about it. Do I say, "Yes, I'm Muslim," just to play along and try to fit into this country where the population is 99 percent Muslim? Or do I say, "I'm a Christian" and see what reaction that potentially unpopular choice provokes?

In a rare moment of courage, I felt inclined not to deny my faith. It seemed downright biblical to proclaim it.

Plus, I was planning to order pork chops and a beer—non-Muslim choices—so I took the risk.

"Nope. Not a Muslim. I'm a Christian."

He paused for a moment. Then with a big smile, indicating he understood me, said "Ah! You are Christmas!"

"Yes," I said, "I'm...well...yes, I am."

It was weird to say out loud, to a total stranger, that I'm a Christian. What made it even odder was that I admitted I'm Christmas, as well.

And that was it for my faith-sharing in the land of Turkey. I know, St. Paul had a bit more success in the country than I did, but, hey, I tried.

The truth, of course, is I'm not big on, "Let me share with you what my personal Lord and Savior, Jesus Christ, has done for me and what He can do for you." Part of me feels bad that I'm not a greater defender of the faith. Other folks constantly preach and teach about God on airplanes, at restaurants, in the men's room, but it's not my style.

I go to church. I say my prayers. I'm Catholic. But I don't actively look for ways to share my faith, especially when I'm eating dinner in foreign lands.

A couple of days later, it was a Sunday in Istanbul and time for Mass. Before leaving on the trip, I had done my research online and knew there was a church a few miles from the hotel. The Church of St. Anthony of Padua seemed like the right fit since I'm Italian—and it had a Mass in English.

Plus, I was sure I'd get lost along the way. And since St. Anthony is patron saint of lost things, I figured I could constantly pray, "Something is lost and can't be found, please, St. Anthony, look around."

So I hit the street and headed out. Whether or not the area was safe for walking, I had no idea. Google Maps gives you directions, not a guarantee of safety.

But with my Mediterranean looks, dark hair, and dark eyes, I figured I fit in. The key was to walk like I knew where I was going and not refer to a map, which is why I had memorized the street names.

Thirty minutes later, I found it. The familiar feeling of walking into a Catholic church let me know that I was home.

"My life really is a paradox," I thought to myself while approaching the beautiful red-brick church. "The more difficult it is to get to Mass, the more I want to go. But when I'm back in New York City where there's a Catholic church two blocks away, another eight blocks, another ten blocks, it's like pulling teeth to get me to go to church on Sunday."

Catholics are required to go to Mass every Sunday as well as holy days of obligation. Although I feel horrible saying it, all this attendance leaves me feeling bored. I rarely look forward to Mass the way it seems I should.

In fact, if it weren't for the Eucharist, I doubt I'd be going to church very often. I know God deserves all honor and glory and praise, but I'd be sleeping in a lot more on Sunday mornings if I couldn't receive the Body and Blood of Christ. That's never boring.

The Church calls the Mass "the source and summit" of the Christian life. But suffering from spiritual ADD as I do, I find listening to the same thing over and over again to be tough. In fact, I'm jealous of folks who want nothing more than to make it to Mass as often as possible. I genuinely think something is wrong with me.

Place me in a foreign country, however, and I have my work cut out for me. It's an adventure, not convenient, a sacrifice. The more the Church asks of me, the more into it I am.

In Turkey that Sunday morning, I chose the second-to-last pew in the back, genuflected, and prayed. As the opening hymn began, I was glad to have found an English-speaking congregation. Even though it's the same liturgy everywhere in the world, it's less participatory when I don't understand a word they're saying.

On the other hand, one thing hadn't changed: I always zone out during homilies. Not the whole thing, but at some point my mind wanders. Sometimes it's because the priest made an astute theological comment. Sometimes it's because he didn't.

Inevitably, I get annoyed and say: "Lino, don't daydream. You can sit through an entire episode of *Jersey Shore* without missing a thing. The least you can do is pay full attention to what's going on at Mass—including the homily—for an hour."

I then realize I'm talking to myself. When I should be paying attention to the homily.

"Focus," I say to myself. "At least your original daydream was because of something the priest said. Now you're just telling yourself not to be distracted anymore."

Eventually I end up yelling at myself. "Quit talking to yourself about the need to quit talking to yourself. Pay attention at Mass."

I finally snap out of it and focus on the homily again. At which point the good Father is usually tying a bow on his theological gift to us: "And if you do that, you'll have peace in this life and eternal life in the next. Amen."

Now I'm even more frustrated. "You moron. All that talking to yourself and you've missed the key to peace now and eternal life later. If you don't start…"

Then I realize everyone else is standing and we're five words into the Creed.

And so it went, there in Turkey.

When Mass was over, I had to remember the directions in reverse to get back to the hotel.

Finding a supermarket along the way, I went in and did some shopping. Much as I take comfort in the Mass being the same everywhere in the world, I take the same comfort in the supermarkets of the earth. I can always buy bread, cheese, Doritos, and a bottle of water.

My few purchases in hand, I went out and sat on the curb to eat my lunch. People couldn't figure out if I was a tourist taking in the strangest of views or a local down on his luck.

The truth? I just didn't want to be eating alone at a restaurant. It's too weird.

18

Big & Tall

I got my first skateboard when I was fifteen. It was cheap, wobbly, and stark white—which also describes many future girlfriends—and it was the last piece of the puzzle I needed to be an official punk.

"So," I said to my friend Keenan, "I think I want to be a punk skateboarder. How do I go about it?"

Keenan was the closest thing I had to an anarchist, even though he was a well-mannered, articulate, law-abiding kid. But he had posters on his walls of The Smiths, Love and Rockets, and Bauhaus. He owned a military jacket. He had long hair in the front, all the way to his eyebrows. He also had a seven-hundred-dollar stereo system complete with turntable, cassette player, and three-foot-tall speakers. And he owned a skateboard. He was as close as I could get.

We'd been friends since the first day of seventh grade, primarily because our last names began with the letter *R* and when the gym teacher lined up the class, we were stuck next to each other. Thus began a friendship. The fact that he, too, had an odd name—guys like Keenan and Lino are meant to be outsiders—was an added bonus.

When I came home from my first day of seventh grade, and Mom asked how my day at the new school was, I said, "I made a new friend. His name is Karen."

"What do you mean *his* name is Karen?" Mom asked. "Karen is a girl's name."

"Oh, you're right," I replied. I wasn't sure if I had made friends with a hermaphrodite or just couldn't remember the kid's name. "I'll get back to you tomorrow with the right name, Mom."

So even though Keenan was the type of guy who had his retirement and 401K plan figured out before we had graduated high school, he was my punk friend. The other thing that gave him street cred was that he didn't go to church.

A few months into our new friendship, we had lunch at a Mexican restaurant. With my mom. After all, punks like us didn't have driver's licenses yet, so if we wanted to socialize, we had to have Mom along. The topic of religion came up.

"Well, you don't believe Adam and Eve were real, do you?" he asked. Keep in mind, he did it with a smile, not the least bit antagonistically. More like the way you ask a Cubs fan if he really thinks his team will win it all this year. You're not being mean; you're just trying to get a sense of what he's thinking.

"Um, yeah, I believe in Adam and Eve. Don't we, Mom?" I had to ask. Religion was the kind of topic reserved for religious education class and Mass, but otherwise as Catholics we didn't discuss it.

Mom jumped in. "Yes, we believe Adam and Eve were real."

Keenan replied, "But how is that possible? Were they just plopped on earth, two fully functioning adult human beings? And if they were the only two people on earth, and they had two sons, Cain and Abel, then where did those guys find women to marry? How did the human race continue?"

I had no answers. I just wanted to eat my chimichanga. At this point in my faith life, I was basically just going through the motions. I thought of God as a big guy in the sky with a white beard and a book listing my sins. I went to church because that's what my parents wanted me to do. I didn't have all the answers, didn't have any of the questions, and didn't really care.

I had no theological answers for Keenan, but it was Lesson One in being a punk: I had to start questioning authority. Or at least asking reasonable, intelligent questions.

The skateboard was all I needed to complete my transformation. During the past year I had grown my bangs long, started buying T-shirts at the local head shop downtown, and looked forward to a summer of hanging out, getting tan, taking naps, and being a punk. I wasn't sure if punks were supposed to be well-tanned and rested, but I wasn't giving that up. It's part of my Italian heritage.

Keenan and I would usually meet at the Sun Ray Shopping Center, about two miles away from each of our homes. It was easy to get to the mall from my house: Just one road with two steep hills. After the long hill down, a small plateau, and then a steep incline back up, you'd reach the shopping mall.

Unfortunately, I hadn't mastered the art of skateboarding, and the hill was a nightmare. I'd see the cool kids going down the sidewalk at breakneck speed on their boards, but I'd inevitably chicken out and ditch mine about ten feet in. I'd land safely on somebody's front lawn and watch the skateboard cruise down the sidewalk without me. The board actually seemed to prefer it that way. It handled much better, didn't veer one way or another, and looked really free. I'd pick myself up and walk down the hill, waving and saying hello to the folks I'd pass.

"Was that your skateboard we saw go by?" a guy would ask.

"Yep, that was mine," I'd say with a shrug.

"That happened yesterday as well, didn't it?"

"Yeah, haven't quite got a handle on it yet," I'd say, looking down at the ground.

"OK, well, see you tomorrow," he'd say, not being mean but getting the sense I may not be learning my lesson.

I'd reach the base of the hill, pick up the board, and not attempt to skate back up. I'd just tuck the board under my arm and walk. In fact, most of my time skateboarding could be better classified as board *chasing* or board *carrying*. Very little skating going on.

Hills weren't my only problem, though. One day Keenan and I were going at a leisurely pace down the street. After just a few kicks, I fell backward, my weight pushed out from under me, and the board went skidding into a busy street just as a city bus drove by. It hit the side of a bus with a thud. The driver wasn't pleased.

At least that's what Keenan told me. I ran away in embarrassment as soon as I'd heard the thud of skateboard meeting bus.

* * *

Perhaps because my parents weren't nearly as amused by these stories as everyone else, they wanted me out of the house. Not permanently, or at least they didn't say so to my face. It was just time for me to get a summer job.

I applied for a bunch of jobs and got one washing dishes at a Mexican restaurant called Chicos (or some hacky name like that). Being a dishwasher was exactly what you'd imagine. After three days, I quit.

Well, I didn't formally quit. I just stopped showing up.

Not wanting my parents to find out, I left the house every day as if I still had a job.

I went to Chico's in case I was being followed, but instead of going into work, I'd walk over to the Hardee's next door and hang out there. I spent most of my eight-hour shift spending—not making—money and watching people who clearly hated their jobs as much as I hated mine.

I still called the job "mine" since technically I never formally quit. As far as my employer knew, I had been eaten by a bear or trapped under something really heavy. If the local news showed up to ask about me, they could say I was an employee.

After a week of hanging out at Hardee's, the No Loitering sign changed to No Loitering, Lino.

I knew I'd have to get a new job eventually so I skateboarded/walked with the skateboard under my arm to the shopping center. The Big & Tall Men's Store had a Now Hiring sign on the front. I swallowed my pride and walked in.

"Hi," I said to Hakeem Olajuwon's taller brother upon entering. "I see you're hiring?"

"Yeah," he said in return, "if you're interested, you can talk to the manager about the job."

That was easy. "Sure," I said.

"OK, let me go get him for you." Then, with a pause, "Actually, it's better if you go to him instead of him coming to you."

Stretch and I walked into the manager's office, and there, behind the desk, was an enormous man. It was like the scene in *Return of the Jedi* when you see Jabba the Hut for the first time.

He barely fit in his chair, and they'd need the jaws of life to pry him out.

"So, why would you like to work at the Big & Tall Men's Store?" he asked.

I was 5'8" and 140 pounds on a good day—a good day being one in which I had twenty-five pounds of coins in my pockets. I could see that he was hinting at the fact that I was neither big nor tall. But I figured you can't hire based on age, race, religion, sexual orientation, height, or weight.

"I just really like clothing, sir," I said. At the time I was wearing a plain white T-shirt and cut-off shorts. A real fashion statement.

"Do you think it'll be to your disadvantage that you're not big and tall?" was his next question.

That's like saying guys won't buy clothes, or take advice, from a guy that's not big and tall. It's illogical. It's like my friends who say priests need to be married because that's the only way priests can relate to married people. Why receive premarriage instruction, the argument goes, or get marital counseling from a guy who isn't married?

Well, hey, if I've got cancer, do I want a doctor who has had my exact form of cancer and survived, or do I just want someone who knows a lot about cancer? To be an expert in something doesn't mean you have had to experience it yourself.

I was determined to make this work. No, I'm not big and tall, but I really didn't want to look for another job.

"No, sir, I think it'll be to my advantage. I'll be an outsider, and I think our customers will appreciate that." Note I said *our* customers. It showed confidence and initiative.

I got the job and became the greeter.

"Hi, can I help you today?" I'd say as Andre the Giant walked in.

The guy would look around, wondering if he had entered the right store. "Uh, yeah, is this the Big & Tall Men's Store?"

"Yes, it is. Let me know if I can help you with any sizes or anything else you need."

Just because I was neither big nor tall didn't mean I couldn't help him get into an XXXXL shirt.

And that was the most ridiculous part of the store. You'd think they'd come up with sizes that wouldn't make the guys feel enormous. An XL at a regular store could be a Small here, and no one would make a fuss.

But, no, there were XXXXXXXXXL Tall sizes. To remind the guys how big they were.

To make matters worse, the same policy applied at Big & Tall that applied at The Gap or Banana Republic: The employees wore the clothing as living mannequins. Because I was slight of figure, I wore XL shirts and pants, the smallest sizes the store carried. The effect was that I looked even smaller than I really was.

I was very self-conscious that I was so short and thin. I tried to gain weight. I put my legs in clamps to stretch them and make me taller. Nothing worked.

Who was more uncomfortable? The big-and-tall guy buying clothes from the skinny-and-short guy? Or the skinny-and-short guy pretending he didn't know the difference between us? I'm not sure.

In retrospect, maybe working at the Big & Tall Men's store helped prepare me for my life as a practicing Catholic because I've never completely felt like I fit in at church. Everyone is either too holy for me or not holy enough.

If a parish is filled with strong Catholics, I try to act extra pious, but I presume they can see through it. I'm insecure in my own faith and feel like I don't fit in. I'm a fraud. I'm apologizing that I'm not Big and Tall and Holy.

On the other hand, if it's filled with lukewarm Catholics, I feel holier than they are and like I'm not being challenged. Now I'm the kid apologizing that I'm Skinny and Short and Too Holy.

I don't seem to fit into the Catholic community, but I'm still looking. More than anything, I envy people who fit in with a good church community. It must be nice. I'm big and awkward when it comes to church.

Oh, and guess who *did* end up fitting into a Catholic community? Keenan. He married a woman who is very devoted to her faith, and so he checked out Catholicism and signed up. Now he's Super Catholic. He, his wife, and his kids are all involved at their church. He's on the parish council and is friendly with the priests and deacons of the archdiocese. He's really found a home in the Church and is a much better Catholic than I am.

Also, he still knows how to ride a skateboard better than me.

19

Adventures in Confession: Part Three

The book is called *Sinner*. There's a running theme: I'm a sinner. And so I go to confession.

But it took me a long time to figure out *how* to go.

So I'm going to do for you what I wish someone had done for me: explain how to go to confession. If you're not Catholic, fine. Don't go. But at least now you'll know what we crazy Catholics are doing in there.

Welcome to the least reverent guide to confession you'll ever read.

After you've committed to the idea of going to confession, you've got to figure out which lucky priest will hear your sins. If you find a parish that has confession by appointment only, move on to the next parish. A parish of three thousand people that offers confession on Saturday from 4:00 to 4:05 might not be where you want to pour out your soul, either. Find yourself a parish that offers confession frequently. Daily is preferable.

Advent or penance services are a great opportunity, but make sure it actually involves going to confession. Don't be fooled by those "communal penance" services that involve thinking about sins but not saying them out loud. That's not confession, that's reminiscing. Also, avoid the

"Let's all write our sins down on a piece of paper and burn them" affairs. Not only is it a waste of time, it's a fire hazard.

If you haven't been in a long time, make sure there isn't a *long* line behind you. I once got stuck behind a girl who was in the confessional for half an hour. Thirty minutes! When she came out she was crying. "Yeah? Well, honey, I've been standing here needing to use the bathroom for the last twenty of those thirty minutes. We're all in pain." But I didn't blame her for not wanting to make an appointment to confess her sins, so I gave her a pass.

There's no shame in deciding you don't want to go to your own parish priest if it's been a long time since your last confession. Keep in mind that it's a supernatural thing going on in confession, though, and the priest will help you through it whether he knows you or not.

After you've determined the where and when, you have to determine the *what*. As in, what horrible ways have you offended God?

First, you'll need an examination of conscience. No one likes examinations, but even if you're dumb, there's no way you can fail this exam.

Going to confession without examining your conscience is like placing a bet on the horses without knowing the odds. Do yourself a favor and get all the information you can beforehand. Go to a Catholic website, or Google "examination of conscience," or look in the back of the church—most churches have pamphlets that'll lay out how to go about examining your conscience. You'll be surprised what a huge sinner you are.

If you have a good memory, there's no need to write down your sins. But if you feel you might forget something, jot a few notes. I'd strongly discourage you from making drawings or diagrams of the acts or sins committed. Also, it's not a credit card application, so don't include your name, address, date of birth, and social security number.

In fact, make it as barely legible as possible. Write it with your foot if you need to. Just make sure the chances are low that anyone else could decipher your chicken scratch.

Once you get into the confessional, here's how it'll go.

Priest: "May the Lord be on your mind and lips so that you may make a worthy confession."

Or he may also begin with, "Yes?" He may just sit there silently and let you begin. There are no hard-and-fast rules. If you hear anything like, "Welcome to Wendy's, may I take your order," you're in the wrong place.

Sinner: "Bless me, Father, for I have sinned. It's been (length of time) since my last confession." If it's been years or decades, there's no need to be precise. Give him a general idea. Who was president or dictator or emperor at the time? If it's going real far back, are we talking the Bronze Age? Stone Age? Give him something to work with. The priest isn't going to be a stickler about details at this point.

Giving him a time frame helps him when he gives words of counsel after your confession. If you've committed all these sins in the last two days, you've got a real problem. If you've done so over the course of a lifetime, it's serious but workable.

Then you let it all hang out. Metaphorically speaking. And my advice? Open strong. Don't say you had a couple less-than-charitable thoughts and then mention killing a few people. Don't bury the lead.

Sinner: "For the sin of missing Mass, which I committed ___ number of times." Again, you can ballpark this. If you skipped out on Mass the last two decades, you can say so rather than doing the math for fifty-two Sundays a year plus holy days of obligation times twenty-four years. And there was a leap year thrown in. He gets the point.

Sinner: "For the sin of ___," and the number of times you committed it. This is for mortal sins, mind you. You're not expected to remember the number of times for venial sins. Those are not deadly so it's OK to confess them without bringing a calculator along.

By the way, it's natural to be embarrassed and ashamed. Unless we're on a reality show, none of us are used to speaking about our darkest, dirtiest activities aloud. But keep this in mind: There's a halfway decent chance the priest is a bigger sinner than you. And don't imagine you're going to tell him something he hasn't heard before—that's the sin of pride. No one has something that original.

The real beauty of the process is that the priest will be excommunicated if he tells anyone what he hears in confession. If he sees you outside, he can't even acknowledge that he heard your confession, let alone mention what he heard.

The priest will give you some words of counsel and a penance. You don't do the penance in the confessional, though. Wait till you leave. He will then ask you to make an Act of Contrition. While it's OK to say "I'm really, really sorry!" it's better to go with a formal one.

Sinner: "O my God, I am heartily sorry for having offended thee…" (look up the rest online) "…to sin no more and to avoid the near occasion of sin. Amen."

The priest then offers absolution. This is cool, because you're almost done.

Priest: "God, the Father of mercies, through the death and resurrection of His Son…" (OK. Let's get to the money line) "…I absolve you from your sins in the name of the Father, and of the Son, and of the Holy Spirit. Amen."

After the absolution, you're forgiven. Your sins are now as far apart as the east is from the west. Oh, and make sure to forgive yourself, too.

King of All Catholic Media

I was always more of a TV than a radio guy, but as a kid I used to listen to a wacky local morning duo pretty much every day. Two guys with the remarkable ability to make some really unremarkable radio. Most mornings they featured a lame contest of some kind.

Proving my own lameness, however, I occasionally would try to win. "Caller number five will win a very special surprise," one host said between songs with lyrics like, "I don't want to work; I just want to bang on the drum all day." I called the line and on the third try, I got through.

"Hi, who is this?" the fake radio voice asked.

"Lino!" I announced triumphantly.

"Congratulations, you're caller number five! You're going to go see Air Supply at the Minnesota State Fair!"

That was the special surprise? Winning tickets to Air Supply was like "winning" the clap.

But I was a kid and didn't know any better, so my mom and I went. The concert sucked out loud. I was hoping the monster trucks at the fair the day before would show up and accidentally run over the group.

A few years later, Mom and I were shopping in downtown St. Paul and ended up on an elevator with one of the morning guys.

"My son is a big fan," she said to him. He looked at me with a cold stare and said, "Oh."

I was offended by his lack of interest in his fans.

"Listen, dude: First, you're a local morning DJ who probably had aspirations for a real career, but this is where you are. Don't be mad at me for your life choices. Second, Air Supply sucks. The seats were right up at the front and you could almost smell the depression coming from the band. Third, if I ever have the slightest bit of the fame that you think you have, I'm not going to treat my fans as poorly as you do."

That's what I should have said, but I was ten. I just stood there.

Years later, after I'd been on television a few years, I was invited to be a guest on their radio show. He didn't remember me, but I told that story just to get it off of my chest. Surprisingly, I wasn't invited back.

Shortly after my appearance, I found out the show was cancelled. My reaction? A cold stare at the person who told me and one word: "Oh."

* * *

Garrison Keillor and his show, *A Prairie Home Companion*, was the first positive radio influence in my life. Garrison is a big Lutheran (I mean *really tall*, though he does seem really into Lutheranism). Lake Wobegon is the imaginary town from which he broadcasts.

My dad was a longtime fan and many Saturdays, while we were cleaning the garage or washing the car, Pops would have *Prairie Home* on the radio in the background.

My dad, the organ-grinder, was also a somewhat frequent guest on the show, and I would tag along and hang out backstage.

Garrison had a deep, rich baritone voice. He spoke slowly. He seemed calm and happy with life. He was the exact opposite of me. I wasn't gonna leave Catholicism and become Lutheran, but if it was faith that gave him that peace—and that voice—it was certainly tempting.

The first time I shook Garrison's hand, it seemed huge to me, more like a baseball mitt than a hand.

"Can I have an autograph, Mr. Keillor?"

"Sure, son," he answered in a voice that was several octaves lower than Barry White's.

He signed my autograph, posed for a picture, and chatted awhile. A good radio dude.

Still, I had no interest in the business.

* * *

The third—and most important—radio influence in my life was Howard Stern. Growing up, I didn't listen to Howard on the radio because his show wasn't syndicated in Minnesota until the mid-'90s, and this was before the days of satellite radio. He would occasionally make appearances on Letterman's show, however, and that's how I came to know about him.

He was funny. He was controversial. He was innovative and pushed boundaries. I liked his attitude, and I liked that he didn't fit in. I especially liked that there was a successful guy in media with a big nose.

I've always been an outsider who doesn't really fit into any group, so guys like Dave Letterman and Howard Stern naturally appealed to me. They didn't seem to fit in either, and the less they fit, the more they rebelled. That's what I did—and still do. So naturally I was attracted to Howard as a personality.

When he wrote books like *Private Parts* and *Miss America*, I could see a lot of myself in his stories. I disagreed with his take on many things—I certainly didn't like what he had to say about religion—but I appreciated his honesty. He could be crude and offensive and yet he could make me laugh till I cried.

His producer, Gary Dell'Abate—they affectionately call him "Baba Booey" on the show—visited the Bahamas in 1996 when I was living in Nassau. He was there for a Super Bowl event called *Real Men Don't Watch Pre-Game*. It was basically Gary and some bikini-clad women. Being the nerd I am, I was there for him, not the girls. I had just finished reading Howard's book, and I wanted a picture with Gary.

"Mr. Dell'Abate," I asked sheepishly, "could I get a photo with you?"

"Sure," he said.

We took the photo, he walked away, and I had this feeling: "I'm gonna work with that guy someday. Not sure how. Not sure why." Keep in mind, I was teaching high-school religion in Nassau, Bahamas—not the fast track to the radio business. It was just a gut feeling that somehow Gary and I—and by extension, Howard—would cross paths again.

This wasn't the universe speaking to me, or some generic energy that Oprah talks about. I also wouldn't claim it was the voice of God, but that's the closest I can get to describing it. A peace came with the idea, like an assurance it would somehow happen.

* * *

In 2004, I'd been working in television for six years, and I started getting some radio offers. The United States Conference of Catholic Bishops gave me a weekly show called *Lino at Large*. A little wacky show airing on Catholic stations across the country.

I tried to be funny, I tried to push boundaries, but it was Catholic radio, after all. I had no intention of making it anything more than a fun opportunity to try something new.

That same year, I was offered a gig doing some fill-in radio work with a woman I knew. It was a morning talk show on a local radio station, and we did a two-week stint hosting it. I genuinely didn't believe anybody was listening, and I wanted to prove it. Maybe it was my inner Stern needing to rebel.

"Hey, folks," I began, "it's 6:00 AM and I'm on a radio station I'd never heard of until I was offered this job. I doubt anyone is listening. Prove me wrong and call in."

We got one call. A guy named Elvis just wrapping up a night shift.

"Dude, why are you listening to this?" I said with a laugh. "And seriously, how much animosity do you have toward your parents for naming you Elvis?"

He responded with surprise. And laughter. "Animosity? No. I like the name."

"Yeah, well, I don't. I also don't like people who name their kids Jesus. What's the thought process there?"

You can take the Catholic out of Catholic media, but you can't take the Catholic out of me.

"Who are these people who saddle their kids with these names? What's worse? Elvis or Jesus? Jesus is the Savior of the world. The Bible says at the name of Jesus every knee should bend on earth, under the earth, and in heaven. Think of the pressure you're putting on the kid."

Silence.

"And then there's the other King, Elvis. By the way, how old are you?"

"Why?"

"I want to know if you're named after skinny Elvis or fat Elvis."

"Thirty-four," he responded.

"Your parents named you after fat Elvis? The guy was practically a whale. That inspired them? Do you have a sister named Mama Cass?"

He hung up. Our only caller of the day.

Later that week, the station ran a contest. The prize was John Mayer concert tickets. This was before he appeared on *Chappelle's Show* or dated Jennifer Aniston, which means I, being a straight male, had no idea who the guy was. The winner came into the studio to claim her prize.

"So what's your favorite John Mayer song?" I asked the moderately attractive twenty-something.

"'Your Body Is a Wonderland,'" she responded.

"Thank you, I try my best. But any John Mayer songs you like?"

I assumed John Mayer wrote a song by that name. Wasn't sure. Went with a joke. Got called into the program director's office.

I knew my approach wasn't going to work at that place, and I wasn't surprised when they didn't offer me a permanent job.

I stuck to my little niche in Catholic media: being edgy when I could, having some laughs, but mostly following the Catholic radio script.

* * *

On June 5, 2006, I got a phone call from the program director of the main carrier of *Lino at Large*. They were pulling my show from the lineup.

"I wanted to say it in person, so you didn't hear it from anyone else. We will no longer be carrying *Lino at Large*. It doesn't fit our programming needs right now."

"Why not?" I asked.

"Well, to be honest, most of our listeners are fifty-five and up. We count on their donations, and your show is geared to younger people. That's not our audience, and they don't give us money."

I figured my career in Catholic media was officially over. I tried pushing limits in morning radio. I tried pushing limits in Catholic radio. I was now pushed out of both.

I got really depressed. The sadness took me by surprise. I had started the job just for fun but had really begun to care about it. I guess I hadn't realized how much it meant for me to work in Catholic radio and how badly I wanted it to succeed.

They say when God closes a door, He opens a window. Usually I want to jump out of that window because I feel I have no more options left. And when you're going through trouble, there's nothing worse than Catholic clichés like "God has a plan" or "When God closes a door, He opens a window."

The phone rang again. It was Pat, my boss with the USCCB.

"Hello?" I said, clearly sad.

"Hey, Lino, it's Pat; how's it going?"

She sounded chipper, which meant she hadn't heard the news that the show had been cancelled.

"I just got off the phone with some folks who are starting a Catholic Channel on Sirius Satellite Radio," she said. "They asked if I knew anyone who might be a candidate as host, and I recommended you. In fact, I'm going to send some of your *Lino at Large* episodes today. What do you think?"

I had become a Sirius subscriber in January of that same year. My buddy Tom, a native New Yorker and long time Stern listener, convinced me to go to Best Buy and purchase a satellite radio so I could listen to Howard in my car.

I listened to Howard over the past several months and loved the show. I was fascinated by satellite radio.

If I hadn't admired Howard, or been a subscriber to satellite radio in the first place, there's no way I would have been interested in this potential job offer. Window? Door? Cliché?

* * *

The company flew me out to New York for an interview, but I really went for the free trip to the city and to see Sirius headquarters.

As I sat in the lobby, waiting for the first job interview of my adult life, Howard Stern walked by. He didn't look over at me and didn't even notice I was there, but I thought to myself, "Huh. I've always kinda thought I'd work with—or around—that guy. And now, well, the opportunity might have come." It felt like a plan was coming together… and not a plan of my choosing.

The interview went well, and we made a demo show.

I prayed a lot that summer to know and do God's will. The truth was, as exciting and interesting as a radio show based in New York sounded, I didn't want to do it. Yes, living in New York had always been a dream of mine, but I had no reason to leave Minnesota. I'd recently bought a condo and the housing market was slowing down, so I'd take a bath on the thing if I tried to sell it. I'd just signed a four-year lease on a new VW Jetta.

I had a television production company that was bringing in plenty of work. In the past year, my team and I had won an Emmy, an Edward R. Murrow, and a Scripps Howard. I had agreed to be the executive producer for a documentary on the environment that might even win the Peabody Award that had been eluding us. Oh, and I had five—count 'em, five—months of vacation a year.

In other words, although I was hurt that no one in Catholic media wanted me and *Lino at Large* was going to be cancelled, I'd be just fine.

If this was God's plan, though, I thought it sucked. It was really, really bad timing.

But I kept praying and kept talking to the folks at Sirius. God's will be done.

* * *

I was at Mass on Labor Day, 2006, when my phone started vibrating in my pocket. I presumed it was a call from Sirius offering me a job. After Mass I went up to a Divine Mercy image of Jesus to pray. At the bottom of the image were the words, "Jesus, I trust in you."

I wasn't sure what the plan was, but I said, "Jesus, I'm gonna trust in you. I know this call is a job offer that will mean I have to move to New York and change my life. But I think it's your plan for me. I trust you."

This was one of the few times in my life when I prayed and found peace. It was a peace, however, that was unfamiliar because it was the peace that comes with doing what God wants, not what I want. A priest friend of mine, Father Joseph, had told me that this job could be a cross I was being asked to carry, that I was being led to do something I had no desire to do.

I left church and listened to the voicemail. "Lino, this is Joe Zwilling. We'd like to offer you the afternoon drive show on The Catholic Channel."

An amazing offer to move to New York and host my own radio show across North America. And my reaction was not gratitude; it was tears.

Every night that week, I cried myself to sleep. "Lord, get me out of this!" I said. Some trust, huh? I was leaving my family, my friends, and my comfortable life, and I really didn't want to.

And perhaps my secret reason I didn't want to take the job? Howard Stern, my radio inspiration, was brutally honest about himself on the air. It's something I admired most about him, and something I'd want to do on my own show.

I wanted to be as honest as possible about my faith, my doubts, and my sins. To let people see my pride, my jealousy, my wrath, my lust. But also see someone who's still trying to fight the good fight of faith.

The audience would see the "real me." The part of myself I revealed only to God. And if I let people see the real me, I'd get rejected by an awful lot of 'em. Which would rip my heart out.

But I took the job and moved to New York to host *The Catholic Guy*.

* * *

Since December 4, 2006, we've done all sorts of crazy things. We've broadcast "Live from Las Vegas" from my hotel room—affectionately named "The Seven Deadly Sins Suite." For Mardi Gras, we did live shows from New Orleans on a balcony overlooking Bourbon Street. We've played "The Catholic Guy Dating Game" with "Catholerettes" appearing to compete for my affections. (I ended up with two girlfriends out of it.)

I've spoken my mind, been honest about my failings, my successes, the Church, and the world. I've made lots of fans. And plenty of enemies.

The publicity we've received includes a July 13, 2008, article in *The New York Times* that said "Rulli's show sometimes sounds like catechism class…but more often achieves the queasy unpredictability of the Stern show itself."

The New York Times compared me to Howard Stern. I must be doing something right.

Last year, Gary wrote a book—*They Call Me Baba Booey*—which landed on *The New York Times* best-seller list. I'd gotten to know Gary in my time at Sirius and invited him on the show.

I had never told him the story about how, when I first met him in the Bahamas, I had a feeling someday we'd work together. I told him now. In some small way, he played a part in helping me figure out God's plan, and I got the chance to thank him for it. I had an inkling back then of where God was leading me, before I could even articulate it.

Over the years, I've heard from countless numbers of people who say they've been affected by *The Catholic Guy*. I don't know if this is where God wants me for the rest of my life. I might quit—or be fired—tomorrow. But God brought me here for a reason.

When listeners call or e-mail to say they've returned to the Church, returned to confession, or even become Catholic, and they say it's because of the show, I, of course, take full credit for these conversions during my contract negotiations.

I realize it's the Holy Spirit, since He's the one working through me, but the Spirit doesn't have rent to pay. I do. So I take the credit.

In fact, at the exact moment I'm writing this chapter, a guy named Dave posted this message on my Facebook wall:

> Lino, my fiancé and I are both Officers in the United States Army, she has been serving on active duty since 2002 and I have been serving since 1991.... I will also be forty Oct 24, 2011—just wanted to say we LOVE your show and you have no idea the impact you have on so many lives...so if you're struggling to find what God is calling you to do, struggle no more...you have found it! May God bless you!

So the show is a success. It affects people's lives. And who gets credit for it? The Holy Spirit. And me. And Howard Stern. I wouldn't be here without him.

21

Theology of the Italian Body

The summer after my freshman year in college, my mom, my dad, and I were in Rome on vacation. It was a blistering hot July day, and my dad and I decided to hit the topless beach. Or, as it's called in Rome, the beach.

"You're not bringing the video camera are you?" my mom asked, afraid she already knew the answer. "I *have* to, Mom," I replied. "We're tourists." So creepy and so right.

Pops and I drove an hour out of the city to a place called Ostia and arrived at the parking lot where our fellow beach dwellers had parked. As we got out of the car, carrying our towels and video equipment, a rare moment of sanity washed over me.

"We probably shouldn't bring the camera, should we?" I said, hoping Pops would put up a fight. "Well," my dad answered, "I guess not. It could get us in trouble." He continued, "Anyway, the camera might be damaged by the sand or water." Very practical.

I put the camera in the trunk, and I actually felt like we did the right thing. In my life, any moral victory needs to be celebrated. Grace builds on nature, and it's not natural for me to do the right thing. It's a chance for God's grace to work on me, nonetheless.

Minutes later, some of the most beautiful bodies in the world were trotting around, and I couldn't believe I wouldn't have this on tape. Instead, I walked around in a (slightly) less creepy fashion: dark sunglasses and a keen memory.

Oh, the Europeans. They appear to be so free and comfortable with their bodies. I wonder if they really are…or if it's just an excuse to try to lust without guilt.

I don't buy it, since they're sinners like the rest of us. Maybe they just act better around topless women, so they get away with it more. "Oh, I'm not sinning. I'm not lusting. I've evolved."

The human body. Sex. Lust. Tough concepts for an adult, let alone for a kid.

* * *

When I was in seventh grade my dad gave me his version of the birds-and-the-bees talk. It wasn't a talk, actually. I was in the basement of the house when Pops came by, threw a book in my general direction, and said, "Let me know if you have any questions."

My first question should have been, "Why did you just throw a book at me?"

Imagine a hybrid between a coloring book, a how-to manual, and a pop-up book. It was horrifying. It kind of explained everything about how babies are made, but with cartoon characters. They weren't cartoon characters I'd recognize, however, like Donald Duck—though Donald would have been a good character for the book since he walks around without pants all day.

Instead, these were just pear-shaped, naked, white people demonstrating how they have sex.

"This is what I do with my wife," the cartoon character would say, addressing me personally with a smile. I'd turn the page and see a rather graphic image of the marital embrace.

"This is how we show our love for one another," the female cartoon character would say, smiling noticeably less than her husband.

I went through a few pages, but I didn't want to deal with it. I decided I'd rather not learn.

The first time I saw the naked form in non-cartoon fashion was in a *Playboy* magazine. This was in the days before Internet pornography, when the only way an adolescent could lust artificially was in magazine form.

"Lino, you're not gonna believe it!" A friend came to my house panting and out of breath, sounding as if he had just seen the Loch Ness Monster.

"You gotta follow me right now," he said. I started to jog slowly behind him, wondering what all the fuss was about.

"Where are we going?" I asked.

"I found a *Playboy* in the woods!" The jog turned to a full sprint. I was sad that NFL scouts weren't timing us.

We arrived in the woods, two guys out of breath for more reasons than one, and saw the *Playboy*. For some reason, the '80s were a time of rained-on porn lying around in the woods. The magazine had been sitting in the elements for months. It was as old and weathered as Andy Rooney's skin.

No words were spoken. We just looked at Miss October: her naked body, her likes, dislikes, and hobbies. We knew it was good, though not necessarily "good" from a biblical point of view. In fact, we knew what we were doing was "bad."

John Paul II once said that the problem with pornography was not that it showed too much, but that it showed too little. Had you told me that at the time, I would have agreed: "The pope is right! Miss October isn't showing enough! And too few photos!"

Of course, that's not what the pope meant. He meant that the problem with pornography is that it shows the body parts—but not the person. Certainly not the soul. It treats human beings as objects—which sums up the way I looked at those women on the beach and the way I look at women every day.

John Paul II developed a teaching known as the theology of the body. It's a complex teaching—don't ask me to explain it—but it emphasizes that the human body is good. Original sin ruins our proper understanding of the meaning of the body, however, and it's up to us to reclaim that which God has given to humanity. He created us good, without a sense of shame in the body. There is shame, however, in misuse of the human body.

* * *

Speaking of which, back to the topless beach: After several hours of looking at the beauty of God's creation, we'd had enough. Also, there are only so many dudes wearing Speedos that I can handle. So my dad and I called it a day.

We got to the car, popped the trunk, and the camera was missing. Someone stole our video camera. They must have seen us get out of the car, wrestle with our consciences, and put the equipment in the trunk.

"Wait a second," I thought to myself. "You mean to tell me that I did the right thing by not bringing the camera…and my reward is to have it stolen? We were punished for doing the right thing?"

I'm not God, but I would have a system of rewarding people on earth when they do the right thing. Especially when they're tempted to do the wrong thing. If it were up to me, upon returning from the beach I would have opened the trunk and not only found the camera there, but a bag full of cash as well. Just as a reward and reminder to continue doing the right thing.

Instead, I've only got memories…

. . . . 22

The Wrestler

The Bible condemns lying and tells us that all our sins are going to be revealed at the final judgment (cf. Matthew 12:36). Well, I've told many lies, big and small, and have many sins to atone for. So let me beat you to the punch when it comes to my lies. You don't have to wait till Judgment Day; I'll tell you about some right now.

* * *

The letterman's jacket worn by high-school and college athletes has long been a sign of accomplishment. It says you belong. You've done something.

You learn a lot about students based on their jacket: the year they'll graduate, their sport, the teams they captain, and so on.

My high school allowed a student to letter not only in football, soccer, or volleyball, but also in debate, chess, or theater.

I was involved in theater as soon as I started high school, and I had accomplished enough on the stage that I had lettered in theater the same way my classmates lettered in sports. In fact, I would become a four-year theater major, and I had a letter jacket to prove it. Suffice it to say, I graduated high school a virgin.

The day I got my jacket, some friends and I headed out to see *Beverly*

Hills Cop II. I figured people would see the jacket and assume I was a stellar athlete. They wouldn't learn the truth unless, on closer inspection of my left sleeve, they saw the masks of happiness and pain.

"Theater?" a girl asked in surprise. "Did you really letter in theater?"

"Yep," I answered in embarrassment.

I felt like a fraud. I didn't deserve a letterman's jacket. I was no athlete. My freshman and sophomore years were spent singing and dancing. The closest I got to an athletic accomplishment was when I performed in *Oklahoma* and had to lift a girl who was twice my size during one of the musical numbers. I nearly threw my back out, but mission accomplished.

The theater jacket went into the closet. I was ashamed that I had wasted my parents' money.

* * *

I had started to have a low opinion of myself in junior high, but high school solidified it.

Freshman year, kids called me *Taco*. This hurt even though I wasn't Mexican. I didn't find it particularly original, either. What kind of insult is *Taco* anyway? It's like calling me *Pasta* because I'm Italian.

Nonetheless, their comments hurt because I care so much about what others think of me. I seek the approval of others—even strangers—more than I seek God's.

I rode the school bus every day and, not being a very popular kid, I would sit quietly and pray. These were not the prayers of a holy person glorifying God. Instead of a rosary or some other devotional, I offered the most selfish, egocentric prayers I could muster.

"God, make me popular. I want to be liked. I'm tired of being made fun of. Please let this day go easy for me." An honest prayer from the heart, but day after day my prayers seemed to go unanswered.

The closest I got to being liked was when a beautiful girl named Kelly befriended me for a few minutes in the early spring of freshman year. I was wearing a Swatch watch that had a large X on it. It was the one thing I owned that was actually kinda cool and trendy.

"I like your watch, Leno," she said. Didn't get the name right, but only a vowel off.

"Thanks," I said, trying to understand why she was being nice to me.

"Can I wear it?"

"Of course!" I said too eagerly. I know money can't buy me love, or at least not for more than an hour at a time, but I thought I'd try.

When I got home from school that day, Mom noticed I wasn't wearing my watch.

"Where's your watch, Lino?" she asked. At least Mom always pronounced my name right.

"Oh, I let a friend wear it for the day," I responded. "She'll give it back to me tomorrow."

The next day at school, Kelly acted like nothing happened. In fact, she acted as if we'd never met.

I never saw the watch again. Mom didn't ask any questions. It was best for all of us.

It turned out that giving away personal items wasn't my path to acceptance. And God didn't seem to be answering my prayers on *my* time schedule. So I needed to follow the road more traveled: I tried to become an athlete.

* * *

Ours was not a particularly athletic family. Nor a religious family. Nor a wealthy family. Nor a successful family.

I recently found a picture of me as a kid, swinging a baseball bat. The odd thing is I wasn't on a team of any sort. I wasn't wearing a uniform. And though I was wearing a baseball hat, it wasn't from any sports team—it was just a generic hat. In other words, I was dressed normally but holding a baseball bat in a menacing fashion. I was mafioso in training.

It was perhaps for this reason that my dad decided to make me more legitimately an Italian with a bat in my hand and had me try out for Little League T-ball. I was eight years old when Pops and I walked down to the Little League field just a few blocks from our house.

I didn't like what I saw—twenty or so kids my age running around like a bunch of maniacs. They seemed way too into it. You can only get so excited at your ability to hit a ball on a waist-high tee.

"I don't like it, Pops." I was more cultured than they were, I determined in my little brain. "I'm out of here."

And we walked away. That was the last attempt at team sports until high school.

My junior year, my friend Charlie—who seemed able to navigate the worlds of sports *and* theater—encouraged me to try out as a wrestler. So I joined the wrestling team.

I got my singlet—perhaps the most terrifying day of poor body image I'd ever experienced—and I hit the mat. Literally. I was on my back so often, pinned there helplessly, I was afraid I'd get mat sores.

One Saturday morning, we scrimmaged with a team from another school. The other team's coach started yelling at me. "Hey, you! Big Nose! How many times you had your nose broken?"

I wasn't sure how to respond. I'd never had my nose broken, but I didn't think it was cool to just call me Big Nose. Before I could say anything, a kid tackled and pinned me to the ground because I wasn't paying attention.

"Wake up!" the coach yelled at me. "Don't let someone blindside you like that! Get back at him! Where's your anger?"

I was pinned by a stranger five weight classes higher than my own, but I wasn't angry at the kid on top of me. I was angry at this coach for saying I had a big nose. And not warning me that someone was gonna blindside me and throw me and my big nose to the ground.

The coach continued to mock me: "You don't know how to wrestle. You look like a stroke victim."

Now the guy was making fun of stroke victims? This is a classy sport.

* * *

I had joined the team at about 130 pounds, and the plan was for me to wrestle at 112. Dropping eighteen pounds wasn't necessarily what a 5'8" stringy kid needed, but being a team player, I did it.

Our first tournament was quickly approaching, and one day Coach made an announcement.

"We need someone to wrestle varsity at 105. Who will it be?"

Considering I was the skinniest kid on the team and only had to lose an additional eight pounds, I raised my hand. "I'll do it, Coach."

I'd go from theater loser to varsity wrestler in the span of one month. And in the span of one week, I'd have to lose a little less than ten pounds.

These were the days before nutritionists advised kids on eating a healthy diet, so my meal schedule went like this:

Breakfast: No food.

Lunch: No food.

Dinner: McDonald's French fries or calorie equivalent.

The day of the match, I headed to the locker room for weigh-in. I had eaten nothing the past two days, and got on the scale: 102. Oops, I was underweight.

Now was my chance to get some fuel before the match. Mom had packed some homemade pizza for me, so as other guys were dry-heaving to remove excess ounces of weight, I was stuffing myself with pepperoni pizza. Great fuel for my body, no doubt.

Before the tournament began, the coach brought all of us together in the adjacent wrestling room next to the main gymnasium.

"All right, boys, let's form a circle and sit down," he said as he turned off the lights.

"I want everyone to be quiet. Calm. Take a deep breath in; now breathe out. Empty your minds." Some of the guys in the heavyweight division were way ahead of Coach on that one.

"Let's pray now. God, give us strength and let us win. Amen."

Beautiful prayer. *Santo subito,* Coach.

"And now," he said in that same prayerful voice, "pin the guy next to you!"

What?

The wrestling room, in complete darkness, turned into a scrum without the ball. Just a bunch of dudes all frantically trying to pin someone.

It was all very primal. Guys screaming things like, "Let's kill 'em!" "Rip their heads off!" and "I hate my stepdad!"

Thirty seconds later, Coach blew a whistle. "All right, on your feet. Get in line from 105 to heavyweight." That meant I was in the front of the line, and I'd be leading my team to victory. "Get out there and win."

The door flew open, and the flood of light was terrifying. After being in the dark for so long, we were like vampires in sunlight. I was the first to run out, but my eyes couldn't adjust. As I tried to get my bearings, I stumbled and tripped over one of the cheerleaders. I picked myself up, offered a quick apology, and continued leading my team to the mat.

We got to our positions and a voice from the heavens thundered. No, not God. It was the PA announcer: "Wrestling at 105, from Hill Murray High School, Lino Rulli." I'm sure he announced the other guy's name too, but it was all a blur.

I met my opponent in the center of the mat. We shook hands. The referee's whistle blew. And I'm pinned within five seconds.

My teammates tried to show support, and I was greeted with faint applause. Coach shook my hand but couldn't look me in the eyes.

There was good news, however. Since there were only two of us in my weight class, my tournament was over. Instead of a day of eliminations, wrestling one guy after another, I could relax on the sidelines and enjoy being a varsity athlete.

"Congratulations, Rulli," Coach said. "You came in third place in your first regional tournament."

"But, Coach," I said, "there were only two of us in this weight class." I'm still fuzzy on the math and how I placed third out of two.

I didn't complain, however, since I got a certificate that said third place. There were guys who walked out of that tournament in eighth place. I took it as a moral victory.

* * *

Over the next several weeks, we had a match or two a week. I had made it as a varsity athlete, even though I was pinned in each of my matches. I had racked up only about thirty seconds of total competition in all, some of those as I ran around the mat trying to avoid my opponent.

The only matches I won were those when the other team didn't have a guy at 105. It was the most shallow of victories to go to the center of the mat and have the ref lift my arm in triumph. One night, as I lay in bed, I decided I had had enough. I didn't want to be a wrestler, I didn't want to earn popularity through sports, but I also didn't want to quit.

So I did what anyone like me would do: I lied.

The previous summer, I had cut my left thumb with a box cutter while opening a crate of bananas. It required ten stitches, and I've got a scar to this day. Because it happened over the summer, and I had few friends, no one knew about the injury or how it happened. I decided my thumb could be my way out.

As I went to sleep that night, I brainstormed my plan. How should I go about fooling the world? Do I say I was in a knife fight? Do I say I was protecting the honor of a woman? I had to come up with a story of heroism, intrigue, and mystery. Most importantly, a story that would place me on injured reserve.

The next day I knocked on Coach's office door and walked in wearing a bandage around my left thumb.

Coach: "Hey, Lino, what's up? You beat anyone up yet today?"

Scared young Lino: "Um, not yet, Coach."

Hairy Coach: "You build an addition to your family house in shop class?"

Untalented young Lino: "Ah, no, Coach. I can't figure out how to use the drill."

Coach, wearing a shirt made of human skin: "You run five miles, bench three hundred pounds, and are ya ready to win your next match?"

Scared young Lino (close to sobbing): "Well, Coach, that's why I'm here. I can't wrestle anymore."

The lie went something like this: I was walking home from the grocery store and saw a car on fire. There was a dog inside, barking and jumping around. The doors were locked and smoke was filling the inside of the car, so I punched my hand through the window.

Coach stopped me at this point. "Why on earth wouldn't you use your elbow? You punched it with your hand?"

"Yeah, well, I don't know. I didn't have time to think. I just...you know...punched."

I then showed him the motion of punching with my left hand. The fact that I'm right-handed, however, became clear. I have no coordination with my left hand, and the flailing motion looked more like a little girl throwing a football.

"Why the hell did you punch it with your left hand? You're right-handed."

The lies were catching up with me already. "I don't know. It was the spur of the moment. Anyway, I punched through the glass, opened the door from inside, and the dog escaped. I had to get a bunch of stitches. The point is, obviously I can't wrestle anymore, but I'd like to still stay on the team with my friends."

He stared at me, waiting for the end of the story.

"What happened to the dog? Or the car?"

"Huh?" I wisely responded.

"You know, the dog? The burning car?"

"Oh." I had forgotten to create this part of the story. Did I adopt the dog? Did the owners show up? Did firemen put out the fire?

"Yeah, a fire truck showed up and the owners returned. Anyway, I can't wrestle anymore but would like to still be on the team, OK?"

It was clear I was lying, but he showed compassion. Coach allowed me to stay on the team, and I came across as a hero to anyone who didn't ask follow-up questions.

Lies are ugly, even when they seem to benefit me. I didn't want to lie, but I didn't want to be a wrestler. Unfortunately, I chose sin over virtue. And have the letterman's jacket to prove it.

23

Progress with Pants

The minute I walk into my home, I take off my pants. At least, I used to.

I've lived by myself for the past ten years, and for most of that time the routine was the same. Unlock door. Open door. Close door. Unzip pants. Remove pants. Place pants on nearest person, place, or thing that will accept said trousers. I'd then unbutton my shirt and remove that, as well. I was now free to move about my apartment.

As you can imagine, after a few days my living room would look like a clothes tornado had hit. "Ransacked" pretty much described the scene. If I ever reported a burglary, the cops would be trying to CSI the place, but they wouldn't be able to figure it out. "There are pants everywhere. What's going on?"

It's not that I'm a nudist. You won't find me in some weird HBO documentary with fellow nudists playing volleyball and grilling meat. And no, I don't have a ponytail.

It's just that when I'm at home, I'm a T-shirt-and-shorts guy who is all about comfort.

When I started going to a spiritual director, the first thing he wanted to do was put order in my life.

"Let's start with your pants," he said, perhaps the first time a spiritual director had ever said that to a spiritual directee.

"You lack discipline, Lino," he continued, wisely rewording the sentiment. "A person who goes home and throws his clothes wherever he wants will never have discipline in the spiritual life. So let's start with that. Hanging your clothes up at night, making your bed in the morning, and being disciplined with little things. The more order and discipline you have in the physical world, the more order and discipline in the spiritual life."

It seemed overwhelming to me. A world where I wasn't putting my pants wherever I pleased as soon as I got home? It's like a place filled with unicorns.

The first night was a challenge. As soon as I got home, I closed the door behind me and began tugging at my belt the way a bird tugs at a worm. But I told myself no. "That's it. No more pants wherever I want them." I went to my bedroom and disrobed the way normal people do and put my pants in a drawer, my shirt on a hanger.

The second night was still a challenge, though a little less difficult. By the end of the week, I had begun to make it a habit. As the weeks went on, it made more and more sense.

More than a year later, I'm proud to say the Lord has broken me from those chains of bondage. In fact, the thought of tearing off my pants the minute I get home is as foreign to me as break-dancing the second I open the door. Just doesn't occur to me.

This lack of pants-on-the-ground might sound ridiculous, but it's progress. It's proof that I can change in little ways. It's order in my life. And that's what I need to see: progress. No matter how small or stupid. Progress.

My life is one big fight. St. Paul says to "put on the whole armor of God, that you may be able to stand against the wiles of the devil" (Ephesians 6:11). Well, how can I fight the devil with my pants around my ankles?

There's a scene in *Animal House* where the guy has an angel on one shoulder and a devil on the other, and that's not far off from the actual spiritual battle every Christian is fighting, whether we acknowledge it or not. And quite frankly, it's tough to acknowledge, because the devil wins a lot.

Every time the devil wins, I'm always tempted to say, "Well, Lino, you suck at the spiritual life. Give it up." I'm quick to be discouraged in the battle. The most difficult thing is not panicking, not saying, "Screw it, I'm not fighting this fight anymore."

So, when I make a little progress, the times the angel wins, I say, "Yay!" and see what challenge is next.

24

The Pope and I

I saw him for the first time in the summer of 1983. I was eleven years old, jammed in a crowd with a bunch of sweaty Italians. We were standing in St. Peter's Square, waving to the man in the white outfit as he drove by us in the popemobile. "Pretty cool," I thought to myself. And then it was time to get some gelato.

Over the years, I saw John Paul II hundreds of times in that square.

When I lived in Rome, my apartment was only a few blocks away. If I had some free time on a Wednesday morning, I'd stop by for the general audience, when he addressed the crowd in the square in front of St. Peter's. If I was around on a Sunday at noon, I'd head over for the Angelus. I could use all the papal blessings I could get.

Some nights I'd just sit in the piazza by myself and see the lights burning on the top floor of the papal apartments. I pictured him working, or praying, or whatever he was doing...and it was cool to know he was there. Just me and him.

He always felt like *my* pope. He was *the* pope. Always had been pope. Always would be. Intellectually I knew otherwise, but in reality I would say the word "pope" and only one man came to mind.

* * *

I was walking home one early evening, and as I passed the Paul VI auditorium I saw a big Mercedes-Benz pull up. I had absolutely nothing to do, so I paused to see who was coming out.

Two guys dressed in black opened the door and John Paul II emerged, looked over at me, and waved.

"Buona sera," he said with a smile.

He then walked into the closest building.

There he was. The pope. Just saying hello. I always got a kick out of seeing him, the Holy Father.

* * *

I was in Rome, in April of 1999, having lunch with my cousin, who was a monsignor at the time. He did the ordering.

"Maialino!" he announced. That's not his nickname for me, that's actually what we were eating: maialino, which means "little pig."

Somehow the topic of the pope came up. Oh, that's right, he brought it up.

"I was speaking to the Holy Father..."

What a name-dropper, huh? See, I don't do that. Robert DeNiro—or Bobby, as we call him—told me long ago, "Lino, don't ever name-drop. It's not appealing."

My cousin continued, "...and I do what the Holy See asks of me."

"Does the pope really know you?" I asked. "Like, by name? By face? If he walked in, would he know exactly who you are?"

"But of course," my cousin answered, somehow hurt that I wasn't sure he was on a first-name basis with the Vicar of Christ.

All I could muster up was, "Wow, that's cool."

"Would you like to meet him?"

"Of course!" I said, not hiding my enthusiasm. "Is that even possible?"

The next day my cell phone rang. It was my cousin: "Be at the Bronze Doors of St. Peter's tomorrow morning at six. You'll have Mass with the Holy Father at seven and a chance to speak with him afterward."

Apparently, you don't question a guy when he says he knows the pope.

"I'm gonna meet the pope!" I yelled to the frightened Japanese tourists who happened to walk by. And then I freaked out because I was once again completely aware of my sinfulness.

"OK, Lino, you've gotta be really holy all day," I said to myself. "You're meeting the pope tomorrow so you better exude a sense of holiness." Yet another feeble attempt at being someone I'm not.

I immediately went to a church and prayed for an hour. Well, I was *in* a church for an hour. I prayed. I talked. I daydreamed. I thought about what I should say to the pope. Do I open with a joke? Can I ask him to bless stuff? Should I ask him what I should do with my life?

That's what I determined to ask: "Holy Father, how do I find out what God wants me to do with my life?" Whatever the pope's answer, what an amazing experience it would be to get advice from JPII! I was set.

The next morning, I showered, shaved, put on my best suit, and headed down to the Vatican.

I arrived at six at the Bronze Doors and saw two Swiss Guards standing there looking at me as if to say, "What does this guy want?" Simultaneously, I'm trying to figure out how exactly to address the situation.

Do I say, "Hello, I'm having Mass with the Holy Father in his private chapel," and just assume they'll let me in? Do I come on more aggressively? "Yo, let me in! I'm going to pray with the papa! You don't know me, son!"

I came up with what will go down as one of the greatest sentences I've ever uttered:

"My name is Lino Rulli, and I have an appointment with Pope John Paul II."

My name is on a list, thank God, and I join the twenty or so other people who have been invited this morning. "Wait a second," I think to myself. "I'm not there for a one-on-one with him? Scam. My cousin isn't as big as I thought."

But it's exciting, nonetheless.

A middle-aged guy in a suit told us to follow him. He led us through a courtyard, up to the top level of the papal apartments, down a long hallway filled with frescoes by Raphael, and into a large room.

The room had three huge windows facing out on the square of St. Peter's. I realized where we were: at the windows where the pope appears every Sunday at noon to pray the Angelus and give his blessing.

My first impulse was to run to the window, open it, and have everyone in the square look up expecting to see the pope—only to see me. If I hadn't been absolutely positive the guy in the suit had a gun, I would have done it.

Plus, I was on my best behavior because I didn't know when the pope would show up. No one tells you a thing. Does he jump out from behind a door and yell, "Pope's in the house!"? I had no idea.

We walked through the large room, into a hallway, and were directed to the left. Now we were in his private chapel. It's a small chapel with about thirty seats in all. At the front, just before the altar, was one of my heroes, John Paul II, kneeling in prayer.

We filed in and sat in silent prayer. I sat in silent awe. "That's the pope, Lino!" I kept telling myself. "That's the pope! I'm ten feet away from the pope!"

I tried to focus on prayer but instead spent my time focused on him. To see him pray was to watch a mystic at prayer. He genuinely seemed to have no awareness of anyone else in the chapel. He looked at peace and in tune with God.

What should have been a wonderful spiritual experience—to pray with the pontiff—became an exercise in selfishness.

"Why can't I pray like that, Lord?" I asked in my typical self-centered way. "I'd like to be holy. I'd like to have power." That's right, I even thought about the "power" the pope has. But people love him, people respect him. That's what I want for my life.

After a few more minutes of him praying, and me staring jealously, he stood up, put on his vestments for Mass, and began. Instead of saying "In the name of the Father, and of the Son, and of the Holy Spirit," he said, "Im Namen des Vaters, und des Sohnes, und des Heiligen Geist."

What the…? I looked around and realized there were some priests from Germany in the group. Turns out the pope offers Mass in the language of choice of the visiting priests.

The entire Mass was a blur, but I remember receiving Communion. "Ah-men," I said, trying to make it sound more like Latin, and not wanting to be singled out as an American.

And though it's the same Jesus, Body, Blood, Soul, and Divinity, in the Eucharist at every church in the world…receiving the Eucharist in the pope's private chapel? I'd never miss a daily Mass.

When Mass was over and the congregation said, "Thanks be to God" in German, the pope went back to the kneeler at the front of the chapel and prayed before the tabernacle. His bishop secretary pointed us toward the door, and the group filed out of the chapel one by one.

Except me.

I wanted this time with the pope to last as long as possible—just me and him. I told myself: "Lino, take this opportunity to pray. You're in a chapel with John Paul II. Just the two of you. After this, you can tell people you prayed in John Paul II's private chapel…privately."

This was amazing. I wished there was a photographer to capture the moment, even though that would mean there were actually three of us, which would ruin the whole story. OK, so I'm glad there was no photographer. Yeah, this was way better. Just the pope and me. And that's when I realized maybe a minute or two had elapsed and I had better leave before I got caught. I walked out, ready to tell the world about my completely unique experience.

Then it hit me: I forgot to pray. I kept telling myself how cool it would be to tell everyone that JPII and I prayed together. Instead, because I'm a moron, I'm stuck telling you I got to *think* about praying with John Paul II in his private chapel.

I made it to the large gathering room and eventually was able to meet the Holy Father. I've never told anyone what we talked about because it's too embarrassing, but I'll do so for the first time right now.

His secretary introduced me: "This is Lino Rulli of the United States."

JPII handed me a rosary, and I said, "Thank you, Holy Father." I then bent forward to kiss his ring. I was so nervous that I went nose-first into the ring and wasn't able to kiss it.

Embarrassed, I lifted my head back up to see him smiling. I was about to say my prepared remarks, but I was in awe. "Thank you, Holy Father," I said a second time. He smiled a bit more, perhaps wondering if I had anything else to say.

A few seconds passed, and he started to walk away.

"Thank you, Holy Father," I said one more time. He turned, smiled, and went on his way.

Me, a guy who gets paid to talk for a living, was speechless in his presence. All I could utter was "Thank you, Holy Father" like an idiot. I didn't get even get to kiss his ring. A complete Papal Fail.

But I still have the rosary. And I got to meet my spiritual hero.

. . . . 25

Brace Yourself

St. Paul wrote that he rejoiced in his sufferings (cf. Romans 5:3). For two thousand years of Christian history, people have found meaning in suffering. John Paul II was a living example of the dignity that can come with suffering.

I'm not there yet. When I suffer, it's usually just an opportunity to complain.

* * *

When I was very young, I didn't question many things. One thing that bothered me, though, was the idea of "starter" teeth. Why would my teeth show up, fall out, and then show up again? I stayed awake at night wondering if the same would happen to my nose. My ears. My personality.

I still remember the horror of a tooth falling out while I was eating lunch. It's the most unnatural thing. You're going about your business and suddenly you see your tooth in your peanut butter and jelly sandwich. It's wrong.

What made it worse was having to dig through my meal—at the urging of my parents—and save lost teeth so that I could make upwards of twenty-five cents should the tooth fairy decide to reimburse me for my loss. It was as if my body parts were for sale.

First the tooth, next thing you know I'm lying in a bathtub full of ice without a kidney. Parents shouldn't encourage their children to sell body parts to strangers. Especially to anonymous strangers who arrive in the middle of the night.

What kind of parents would allow someone to enter their child's bedroom while the toothless child sleeps, and take said tooth in return for a quarter? Why does the fairy want all these teeth? What nefarious things is this fairy doing with children's teeth? And is it still politically correct to refer to this tooth hoarder as a fairy?

As I entered sixth grade, my permanent—that is, not for resale—teeth had come in. I intended to keep them. But in sixth grade I lost my head, and my teeth, over a girl.

Her name was Sarah. She was in the fifth grade, and she was perfect. She really looked like Snow White. She was my girlfriend—and way out of my league. Yes, even as a ten-year-old, I knew she was out of my league.

It was an odd relationship. We rarely spent time as a couple, never went to a movie together, never shared a lunch or dinner. We occasionally spoke on the phone. Though our houses were only two miles apart, our main means of communication was letter writing. It was as if we were living during the Civil War.

> *Dearest Sarah,*
> The men are tired. We are running out of rations. The winters are cold. But my heart burneth for you…
> *Yours,*
> *Lino*

She sent me a postcard when visiting her grandparents in Florida. The card shared little information beyond the weather and temperature, but she ended it with, "Love, Sarah." That's all I needed. A non-family member loved me.

One of our rare public meetings took place at the school's spring concert. My mom brought me and was sitting faithfully in the audience waiting for my violin concerto. My dad, quite wisely, wasn't there. The idea of going to his son's school concerts was reason enough for him to get a second job. I don't blame him. I'd much rather take a second or third job than listen to a ten-year-old play *Für Elise*.

Minutes before the concert, Sarah and I were in the long corridor leading to the concert hall (otherwise known as the school gym). Every girl likes a musician, and I imagined that after I wowed everyone with my performance, she and I would cement our love with a kiss. Or holding hands. Or doing something in public.

Shortly before curtain time, my friend Ernie came up to hang out with us. Ernie and I were about the same size, except he was taller, stronger, and bigger than me. He had Brillo-Pad curly hair, freckles, and green eyes. A friendly kid, but with a look in his eyes that tells you he might steal something.

Ernie, like any red-blooded American boy, was attracted to Sarah. And like any other human on the planet, he could see that she was out of my league. Thus, he and I exchanged witty, masculine conversation to win Sarah's favor. As we joked around, Ernie pushed me from behind, simultaneously putting his foot out to trip me.

Sadly, balance has never been my strong suit, physically or mentally, and I went face-first into a wall. Were it to happen today, my giant nose would be broken. This being pre-puberty, and pre-giant nose, I went face-first. Specifically, teeth-first.

My front tooth was gone and blood was pouring out of my mouth like an open fire hydrant. I walked into the concert hall (school gym), and my mom saw her son's new white shirt now red with blood. My permanent tooth? Gone. Didn't even get any money for it.

Thus would begin a period in my life known as: Lino goes through puberty. Without a front tooth.

* * *

I would now have the opportunity to unite my sufferings with Christ. This was my chance to grow in holiness. To offer it up, as my grandmother would say, without explaining how to go about it.

"You've got to offer it up, Lino," she'd say.

"How do I do that, Grandma?"

"Ah, what the hell, the pizza is burning! [Yelling to my grandfather] Damn it, Armando, the pizza is burning! What the hell are you doing in the kitchen?"

Good talk.

I never learned how to offer up my sufferings for others, but I knew it was the right thing to do. I did, however, take full advantage of my Italian heritage to complain about my suffering. And in my defense, my orthodontist gave me something to complain about.

I called him Dr. Barker because I thought he looked a little like Bob Barker from *The Price Is Right*. He had three dental hygienists who could've passed for the real Barker's Beauties. The doctor would ask for an instrument to jam into my mouth, and one of his Beauties would present it as if she were revealing a new toaster oven. They weren't very good at whatever it is they were supposed to do, but they looked great. Their sultry permed hair, formfitting hygienist's outfits, willingness to be around me and my open mouth—it was all very exciting.

A professional, licensed orthodontist would probably suggest I get a false tooth for that gap in the middle of my mouth. Have it glued in with a bridge and that would be the end of it. It was my *front* tooth that was missing, after all, so let's go with the quick fix. But not Dr. Barker.

Nope, this guy had a better idea. This orthodontist with dreams of steel would soon be the talk of the dental community.

The plan was simple: He would drag all my teeth over one. After he was finished, the tooth that used to be just next to my front tooth would get capped. And that would be my front tooth. Confusing, right? So I had some questions.

How long would it take to pull these teeth over one spot? He wasn't sure. Never tried it before. How much would it cost? No idea. How much pain was involved? He had a pretty good idea, but didn't want to tell me.

This would put him on the dental map. He'd be in the dental hall of fame.

Every month I would report to Dr. Barker and his Beauties, and he would slowly pull my teeth over. Not surprisingly, the teeth were less than thrilled. They were permanent—not for resale and certainly not open to relocation. It would be easier to displace some Israeli settlers than convince my teeth it was time to move.

But move they would. Their reluctance just meant Dr. Barker had to pull on the metal braces all the harder. And along the way, he took photos every month for his future dental conferences.

* * *

Throughout the centuries, lots of people have suffered all sorts of pain because of the faith. They have accepted it willingly, even joyfully, because they found meaning in it.

In the second century, a guy named Tertullian wrote: "The blood of the martyrs is the seed of Christianity." The witness of the Christian martyrs actually helped Christianity flourish. People said, "Hey, that dude Ignatius of Antioch is being eaten by a lion and seems OK with it. I should find out more about this religion he's willing to be killed for."

St. Bartholomew was skinned alive. That would suck. But Bartholomew wouldn't renounce his faith in Jesus Christ.

St. Stephen was stoned to death. I tried that, technically, in college. I didn't die, I just gained a lot of weight due to the munchies.

St. Cecilia was beheaded. Paintings typically depict a man with a sword accomplishing that in one clean cut, but it wasn't always that easy.

Tradition has it that a deacon named Lawrence was grilled alive. Halfway through his roast he said, "Turn me over, I'm done on this side." To this day, he's the patron saint of comedians. No joke.

Two thousand years of Christian martyrs—and all they had to do was renounce their faith in Christ and they wouldn't have been killed.

The early Christians didn't complain about their sufferings. I, on the other hand, was complaining about my braces when the only blood I would lose and pain I would endure was for straight teeth. I might have renounced my faith just to avoid Dr. Barker.

Truth is, I'm sad to say that if you threatened to kill me because of my faith I'd reject it, but have my fingers crossed. Internally, I'd be saying, "Lord, I don't mean this!" But externally, I would be renouncing Christ.

But I never prayed for God to help me offer it up. I never asked God to allow my sufferings to be for the benefit of the souls in purgatory or for the sufferings in the Body of Christ here on earth.

I was resolute about *not* offering it up, because offering it up meant accepting it. And to accept it meant that what I was dealing with was real. It meant I accepted God's plan, that His will, not my will, be done.

I prefer the delusional little world I created where things will change and I don't accept reality. Because if I choose to find meaning in suffering, it means there *is* suffering. And despite all of human history pointing to the fact that, yes, suffering does exist, I have yet to really acknowledge suffering exists. I'd like to pass on that.

Not a very mature way to look at the world, but the first step in getting closer to God is identifying my weaknesses, right?

* * *

Sarah and I broke up shortly after the loss of my tooth. I saw her a few years later when, to my dismay, we went to the same high school. She was a freshman; I was a sophomore. Though I was the upperclassman, she was still cooler than me.

She was more beautiful than ever, a cliché cheerleader dating a cliché football player. It was a Catholic school and we wore uniforms, but she knew how to make it look good. Mine just sat unpleasantly on my skin like a rash.

One day she walked by my locker and said, "Hi." It was the type of "hi" a really wealthy woman says when she accidentally makes eye contact with a beggar as her Benz is stopped at a red light. She was uncomfortable. So was I.

At the end of my sophomore year, four years after losing my permanent tooth, the braces were removed. Dr. Barker put a temporary cap on my new front tooth. The experiment was over. We said good-bye, and he reminded me I'd need to come back in two years to have the cap replaced with a permanent one.

That was 1987. I haven't been back since.

26

Golden Idols

The Old Testament warns against graven images and golden idols in our lives. That was written thousands of years ago, of course, and no one has golden idols anymore. Except me. My golden idol? The Emmy Award.

I got into television in 1998. I was hosting a Catholic television show called *Generation Cross* designed for the eighteen-to-thirty-four-year-old demographic. Or what the Church calls young adults. The idea behind the program? "A Catholic TV show people would actually watch." That was our pitch: religious television that didn't suck.

We used the line—A Catholic TV show people would actually watch—in some of our advertisements. Friends who work in Catholic television would call and say, "Well, we, we, you know, we, uh, we create television we think people actually watch, Lino." And I said, "Yeah, old people." Always winning friends. That's me.

We were trying to do something different with *Generation Cross*. The show featured me doing funny things like cooking or rock climbing with priests, ice-skating and golfing with nuns. You'd learn about faith and have some laughs.

We had been at it for two years but, as you may have sensed by now, I'm always seeking affirmation. When you tell me that Jesus loves me and that should be enough, I'm the guy who says, "It's good that He loves me. It's not enough." Having strangers love me? That's enough.

Over time I've noticed that some of my insecurities are rooted in my need to feel special and unique. In my mind, it goes like this: *Jesus loves everyone. I know that. He died on the cross for my sins. OK, I'm feeling good about myself.* Then I go to a carnival, see a carney with no teeth, a silver hook for a hand, and weird face tattoos, and think: *Jesus died on the cross for that guy as much as for me? I'm feeling less special right now.*

At any rate, when it came to my television work, it wasn't about ratings or having people recognize me. It was about the Emmy Award. In addition to the hole in my heart that can only be filled by the applause of strangers, there's the part of my heart that can be filled only by the applause of colleagues. I knew that would complete me.

But I also knew it was a long shot. Back in the 1950s there was a guy named Archbishop Fulton Sheen who had a TV show on a major network. He won an Emmy for his work. That was my goal: to be the first person since Fulton Sheen to win an Emmy while hosting a Catholic TV show.

I put in my application and waited—and prayed. Several months later, the nominations were announced, and I was nominated for Program Host—Non-News. A rather specific category, but that gave me an even better chance: A host of anything but a news program.

Every night, I spent a great deal of time explaining to God why winning the Emmy would be good for me—and good for Him.

"Lord, I thank you for this day," I normally began my night prayers. Then I got down to business: "It would be *sooo* good for me to win an Emmy, to show the world that Catholics in media are just as talented as everyone else. If I win, we'll get good press, which means more viewers to the show, which means more Catholics. People will come back to the

Church because I won an Emmy! And that's what you want God, right? You want people back in the Church, don't you?"

When other people start telling God, the creator of the universe, what's best for Him and how He'll benefit from their plans, I see through it and laugh. When I do it, I'm blinded by my own stupidity. It was pretty clear, though, that the Emmy Award was all about me no matter how much I claimed it was about God. I wanted this so bad. It would affirm me. It would say that I was good, and that my peers agreed.

About a week out, however, I really started to detach and say, "Either way, Lord. If I win, great. If I don't, that'll be fine, too." I was probably just tired of spending so much time praying.

Emmy night. Open bar, the booze is flowing, and—"The Emmy goes to Lino Rulli."

I went to the podium, thanked God, thanked myself, thanked the bartender. If I'd known it was an open bar I'd have prepped a speech in advance. The rest of the night was a blur of people I didn't know winning awards that weren't as important as mine.

Later, in the men's room, I saw one of the guys I beat. He said, "I remember how excited I was when I won my first Emmy…" OK, a little bit of a shot to remind me he's been here before, but that was fine. I went outside and had a cigarette. Because anytime something good in my life occurs, why not try to shorten my lifespan to keep these memories to a minimum?

I prayed: "Thank you, Lord. I know how small I am, how I made this a golden idol, but I'm grateful you allow good things to happen to me even though I don't deserve them. Well, I have the talent. I don't mean I didn't deserve it…" There I was, making it about me again.

"But I do thank you, Lord. And I do hope this will give glory to you."

Afterward, a bunch of us went to a bar and celebrated, and I crashed at a friend's place.

The next morning, on the drive home, Bruce Springsteen's song "No Surrender" came over the radio.

We made a promise we swore we'd always remember.
No retreat, baby, no surrender.
Like soldiers in the winter's night with a vow to defend.
No retreat, baby, no surrender.

I listened to the lyrics, thinking about the fight I'd waged the past several years. For reasons I can't quite figure out, I wanted this Catholic TV show to be successful. I wanted to prove to myself, and others, that I was good enough to compete—and beat—mainstream broadcasters.

There were lots of days I wanted to quit. Lots of days it seemed it was a complete waste of time to do a Catholic TV show. But I kept going. I kept fighting. I'd made a promise to myself that I'd do everything I could to win that Emmy Award. I wouldn't give up till I did.

I wanted that award so badly, and I finally got it. I started to cry.

I pulled the car up to my house, went inside, and went to my bedroom. I got down on my knees to thank God and started to cry again, this time the big can't-catch-your-breath type of tears.

"I'm a sinner, God. I don't deserve anything you've given me. I'm sorry for all the times I've failed you, and all the times it's been about me instead of you. But I'm just grateful you've forgiven me. I'm grateful you love me. And please give me the will to keep fighting. I know that stupid Emmy shouldn't mean anything to me, but it means I did a good job. It means my peers said, 'Well done, Lino.'"

I became aware, at that moment, of the real driving force in my life. The fight I won't abandon, even though I keep sinning, is the fight for heaven.

At the end of my life, I want to be able to say I fought the good fight, I finished the race, and in spite of everything—including getting in my own way—I made it.

Instead of "The Emmy goes to Lino Rulli," the only words that really matter to me are from Jesus.

I want to hear Him say: "Eternal life goes to Lino Rulli. Well done, good and faithful servant."

Even a sinner like me can hope for that.

Acknowledgments

There are a lot of people I'd like to thank.

First of all, I want to thank my personal Lord and Savior, Jesus Christ… Sorry, scratch that. I didn't win the Super Bowl, I just wrote a book. I'm a Catholic—thanking God goes without saying.

I dedicate *Sinner* to my mom and dad. Everything I am, for better or worse, is a result of you two wacky kids getting together. My very existence is proof of what was wrong with the late '60s and early '70s.

But if it weren't for my mom and dad, I wouldn't be writing this. No, seriously, if they didn't insist on spending my future inheritance so reckless and foolishly, I wouldn't be stuck writing a book just so that I have some sort of nest egg when I retire.

I love you both very much. And Pops? Sorry I make fun of you more than I do Mom.

I'd also like to thank all my friends who've been with me over the years. From grade school, junior high, and high school. My college and grad school friends. My friends in the Bahamas and Italy. My friends in Minnesota and New York. The folks who worked with me on *Generation Cross*, *Lino at Large*, and *The Catholic Guy*.

I'm tempted to create a long list of names here, primarily to keep a few friends *off* the list to drive them crazy. There are some people I do want to thank, though, because they've helped me with my career, but their names don't appear in this book: Father John Forliti, Mark Croteau,

Father Peter Laird, Dave Dennison, Father Joseph Johnson, Bill Arnold, David Schechter, Tom Aviles, Jay Clark, Cardinal Edward Egan, Jim McClure, Lou Ruggieri, Maureen McMurray, Father Jim Chern, and Father Rob Keighron.

Of course, I want to thank my listeners. You encouraged me to get over my fear of failure and actually write this thing. If the book turns out to be a disaster? I'm blaming you.

And if you are neither related to me, nor a friend, nor coworker or listener, I thank you as well. Whether you bought the book, received it as a gift, found it in the garbage, or stole your copy: Thanks.

Although she didn't want me to mention her, I'm grateful to my editor, Cindy Cavnar, formerly of Servant Books, who has been pursuing me to write a book for years. And I do mean years. This is the actual e-mail of our first correspondence:

> 2/24/06
>
> *Lino,*
>
> Would you like to talk about a possible book project? I know you can write jokes, but I don't know if you have a broader writing background. You do have the humor, the edge, the faithful Catholic attitude and the desire to evangelize young adults. I like that combination although it might not translate into a book. But who knows, it might.
>
> If you'd like to talk, please send me your phone number and suggest a time.
>
> Thanks,
>
> *Cindy Cavnar*

Only now, more than five years later, will we find out if my combination of talents "translates" into a book. If it works, you can thank her.

I'm also grateful to Servant Books for letting me get away with murder on my contract. Please don't let other authors get the same deal or I won't feel special anymore.

Strangely, I'd like to thank Doubleday Publishing, as well. I realize that's odd considering that Doubleday didn't publish this. But a few years ago I received an email from someone there asking about my interest in doing a book with them. It was the ensuing conversations that really encouraged me to finally write: knowing other people wanted me.

I'd especially like to thank me. Because honestly, without me, none of this would have been possible. Though I wish I had hired a ghost-writer...Thank you, Lino.

* * *

About the Author

LINO RULLI hosts *The Catholic Guy*, a three-hour daily show heard across North America on SiriusXM Satellite Radio. In addition, the three-time Emmy winner has worked in television since 1998, earning some of television's highest awards in journalism. Which makes the fact that he works in Catholic radio even more bizarre.

Lino is a popular speaker who has given talks nationally and internationally. In 2008, he spoke in front of 25,000 people for Pope Benedict XVI's Youth Rally in New York. Never before had such a large group of people collectively not wanted to see Lino.

He holds a bachelor's degree in communications and a master's degree in theology. He has lived in Italy, the Bahamas, and Minnesota and currently lives in New York City with nineteen cats and a medium-sized ferret named Mr. Jenkins.